Core Concepts

For Snowsports Instructors

P9-BIO-204

Credits

EDUCATION DIRECTOR
Linda J. Crockett

LEGAL COUNSEL
Peter W. Reitz

DESIGN & PRODUCTION
EnZed Design

ILLUSTRATIONS
Tim Lee

PRINTING & PREPRESS
American Web, Inc.
GraphX, Inc.
Sprint Press, Inc.

ISBN 1-882409-21-3

Printed in the United States of America
♲ Printed on recycled paper

Table of Contents

Acknowledgments v

Introduction 1
Our Mission 1
Historical View 2
Core Concepts 2

PART 1 Relationships, Experiences, and Learning

CHAPTER 1: KNOWING YOURSELF 5
Why Do You Want to Teach? 6
Be Honest with Yourself 6
Connect with Your Students 7
What Is Your Picture of Success? 8
Learn about Yourself 8

CHAPTER 2: DISCOVERING YOUR STUDENTS 9
Mental Processes 10
How the Brain Works 10
Sensory Contribution 11
Development of Mental Processes 12
Learning Styles and Preferences 13
Multiple Intelligences 14
Emotions and Learning 15
Emotional and Social Development 15
Play 16
Memory 16
Summary–Emotions and Learning 17
Learning to Move 17
Anatomy 101 17
Physics 19
Physical Growth and Development 20
The Aging Process 21
Gender Differences 22
Summary–Learning to Move 22

CHAPTER 3: COACHING YOUR STUDENTS 23
Developing Trust 24
Confidence 25
Teacher Expectations 25
Breaking the Ice 26
Interpreting Behavior 28

Getting the Learner Involved 29
Previewing 29
Summary–Developing Trust 30
Assessing Movements 30
Where Do We Want to Go? 30
Where Are We Now? (What Do You See?) 31
How Do We Get There? 33
Summary–Assessing Movements 34
Working the Learning Environment 34
Maslow's Mountain 35
Need for Safety and Security 35
Need for Belonging 38
Need for Self-Esteem 38
Effective Communication 39
Creative Practice Time 42
Group Handling Skills 42
Teaching Activities 43
Levels of Understanding 44
Feedback 44
Make Sure Your Feedback is Welcome 44
Make Sure the Feedback is Meaningful 45
Debriefing and Closure 45
Build Your Own Teaching Model 46
Evolution of a Practice 47
Brain Stretchers 47
Steps for Building Your Own Model 48
Mental Model Credo 48

CHAPTER 4: WORKING RELATIONSHIPS 49
We're All In This Together 50
Joining the Team 52
Be Aware 52
Make Contributions 52
Acknowledge the Contributions of Others 52
Resolving Conflicts with Customers and Team Members 53
Styles of Conflict Resolution 53
Be Positive 55
Identify the Source of Conflict 55
Stay Focused on the Real Issues 55
Summary–Resolving Conflict 56

PART 2 Responsibilities

CHAPTER 5: CREATING LASTING MEMORIES...59
Why People Don't Come Back 61
You Make the Difference 62

CHAPTER 6: THE MOUNTAIN ENVIRONMENT...63
Managing Risk in the Mountain Environment 64
Your Responsibility Code.......................................65
Choice of Terrain 65
Pacing 67
Preparedness 67
Avalanches 69
Coaching Proper Lift Procedures 70
Coping with Accidents and Injuries.......................71
Summary–Your Role in Managing Risk 71
Sharing the Mountain Environment 71
History..72
Climate and Weather 72
Wildlife..73
Plant Life...73
A Word on Summer Activity 74
Sustainable Slopes 74

CHAPTER 7: PROFESSIONAL DEVELOPMENT...75
Personal Mastery 76
Getting Started...76
Carrying Through...77
Fitness..78
Equipment 79
What is Optimal Gear?..80
Customizing Your Gear 80
Revitalizing Your Career..81
Appreciating Diversity 81
A Final Thought on Renewal 84

REFERENCES..85
Bibliography 85
Websites 86
Online Appendix 86

GLOSSARY..87

INDEX 93

Acknowledgments

AUTHOR
Maggie Loring, Education Steering Committee

CONCEPT & DEVELOPMENT
Publications Task Force, Ray Allard, Chair
Education Steering Committee, Victor Gerdin, Chair

REVIEWERS
Gwen Allard, Ray Allard, John Armstrong,
Mermer Blakeslee, Katie Fry, Victor Gerdin, Megan Harvey,
Dave Merriam, Joan Rostad, Kim Seevers, Shawn Smith,
Rob Sogard, Brian Spear, Weems Westfeldt, Sherm White,
and Debra Willits

PRODUCTION MANAGEMENT
Rebecca Ayers

PHOTO LOCATIONS
California—Mammoth Mountain
Colorado—Aspen Highlands, Breckenridge, Snowmass,
Steamboat, and Winter Park
Vermont—Stowe

In 1999, PSIA-AASI asked all of its national committees
to present a list of essential topics to cover in a comprehensive snowsports instruction manual. The list—roughly
in order of importance—is shown below. In glancing at the
list, it is easy to see that an in-depth discussion of these
topics could fill an encyclopedia!

- Human development; behavior
- Movement; patterns, analysis, biomechanics,
  anatomy, alignment
- Teaching theory; art, styles, models, delivery
- Adaptive, ADA, children's issues pertinent to
  all disciplines
- Age issues (seniors, kids)
- Environmental awareness, ecology
- Learning theory, learning styles
- Service theory, customer service
- Communication skills, developing relationships,
  group dynamics
- Equipment knowledge, (in general)
- Professional, personal, business development;
  leadership; decision-making
- Sales, marketing, PR
- Creating/managing a learning environment;
  building trust
- Creating positive experiences, goals, motivation
- Fear
- Physics
- Professionalism
- Risk awareness; safety
- Specific models (teaching, development, etc.)
- Sport physiology
- Sport psychology
- Building progressions
- Class handling
- Clothing, dress
- Definitions, glossary, area facilities and services
  defined/explained
- Ethics
- Exercise, conditioning
- Fitness, nutrition
- Foreign languages, culture
- Gender issues
- General descriptions of all mountain sports
- History
- Lateral learning
- Listing of other resources
- Medical, first aid, EMT issues
- Multiple intelligences
- Resort business
- Sport science
- Teaching for transfer
- Technical trends
- Terrain use
- Using multimedia teaching tools

This manual is the centerpiece of a new cycle of publications for all snowsports instructors: alpine, nordic,
and snowboard. It contains information for understanding how people learn and using that information to
tailor snowsports experiences for guests. Sport-specific
technical information (learning to turn or slide or glide)
is covered in companion pieces to this manual. This
reinforces the idea that relationships, experiences, and
learning are significant parts of what people are seeking
in snowsports. The ability to perform the sport itself
expresses the quality of these initial building blocks.

Introduction

Our Mission

The purpose of this manual is to help teachers of all snowsports effectively share their passion for the sports they love. The core manual explores the foundation of the learning experience: the connections between the learner and the teacher. Building and fostering meaningful relationships and experiences with students and guests, combined with living up to the standards of professionalism, form the cornerstone of our success as individuals and as an industry.

How did I get so hooked on teaching? Well, I guess I just feel great when I'm teaching something I love. And I know I can help people learn. Not just about skiing or riding, either. Like this one woman I remember who conquered her fear of a certain slope, or the kid who made his first group of friends (he was a teenager!). I can help people feel a sense of accomplishment and a joy for the sport.

Actually, it was a combination of many small events that led me in this direction. Sliding down a mountain has always been something I felt good about. Just being outside in the cold when other folks are wishing it was summer gives you a sense of accomplishment. Conquering the combination of the elements and the terrain is satisfying, yet provides continuing challenges. Just because you can do it today doesn't mean you will be able to tomorrow. You can't take it for granted.

And then there's the social part. Really cool people ski and ride. I mean REALLY COOL! People who come to the mountains only once in a while can spot someone who lives here in a second.

There's a way of dressing, acting, and moving through life that brands you a mountain-lover. As a kid, I looked up to those people and aspired to be one of them. Now, I help other people get there. But it's selfish, really, because the more people I turn on to it, the more cool people there are to hang out with, hit the slopes with, talk about skiing, riding, and teaching with, and learn from.

Welcome to the world of snowsports teachers! If you are reading this, chances are that you are either about to begin sharing your love and passion for winter sports with others or are looking for a renewal of your focus on teaching winter sports. Over the years, PSIA-AASI has developed ever newer and better ways to organize and present the skill-sets necessary for enjoying our sports.

Proficiency in snowsports instruction takes more than just a good training program and years of experience. It takes a love of meeting new people, confidence in one's abilities, awareness of being part of a team, and a passion to share the love of recreating in the mountains. By "participating" in this manual, you will discover the importance of developing relationships and experiences that set the stage for your students to learn a lifelong sport and gain a lifelong appreciation for the mountain environment.

If you are a new teacher, this guide will help you discover the resources you will need to be successful. If you are an experienced teacher, this guide will help you identify new areas to explore, hone your relationship-building skills, and continue to grow as a professional.

Historical View

"Skiing is more than a sport, it is a way of life."
— OTTO SCHNEIBS
   DARTMOUTH SKI TEAM COACH, 1931

Early writings about skiing describe it as a "curious mode of Scandinavian transportation." We know that the origins of skiing go back some 4,000 years, but it was not until the middle of the 19th century that skiing evolved into a sport, as an inevitable outgrowth of the human spirit for adventure and challenge.

Pioneer racers challenged themselves and others to ski faster and with more precision. The same type of spirit for competition and personal excellence inspired early ski jumpers, cross-country racers, snowboarders, freestylers, and so forth.

The mystique and romance involved in climbing mountains only to slide back down attracted creative individuals who began to envision a tourist industry that would provide access to the mountain environment for everyone.

Equipment from Skiing's Humble Beginnings

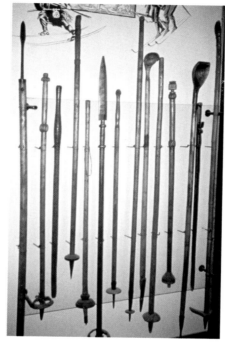

PHOTOS BY HERB DAVIS

Friedolf Nansen, one of the early explorers, crossed Greenland on skis. Nansen had an almost mystic reverence for the sport. He is quoted in *Skiing Magazine's Legends of American Skiing*: "On a brilliant winter day, one binds one's skis and takes one's way out into the forest. Civilization is washed clean from the mind and left behind with the city atmosphere. One's whole being is wrapped in one's ski and surrounding nature. There is something in the whole which develops the soul and not body alone."

This spirit of adventure and the continuing search for excitement has stimulated a continual evolution of snow-riding tools. These include skis and snowboards of all shapes and sizes, twin tips, snow-bikes, shaped telemark skis, split boards, skating skis...the list goes on. All of the tools past and present have several things in common—born of the common need to float, glide, track, and turn on the snow. Each has a base and two edges, a tip (or tips), and a tail. They all have some type of sidecut or shape, and they all flex or bend. They also require their human users to move their bodies in a way that creates and controls the forces needed carve a turn, negotiate a mogul field, initiate a trick, or simply stop.

The similarities among snow tools lead us to explore the most common aspect of all: the learning environment. At the heart of it all lie the excitement of bringing new people to the sport we love and the desire to enhance and enrich the experiences of those already engaged in the sport. Our mission is to continue to evolve the techniques, practices, and philosophies for accomplishing these goals.

Core Concepts

"A teacher affects eternity; he can never tell where his influence stops."
— HENRY ADAMS
   QUOTED IN PHILLIPS, 1993

This guide is designed to serve as a resource for teachers and ambassadors of all snowsports. It is to be used in conjunction with the sport specific manuals, which delve more deeply into technical skills and approaches to teaching. The core is the most important part of something, the heart of the matter. For teachers of snowsports, the core represents the nucleus of all that we do in our lives and our jobs. Regardless of the tool(s) we choose, we find similarities and shared knowledge. We hope that you consider this as a living document that evolves, and sparks and inspires further exploration.

Part 1
Relationships, Experiences, and Learning

Teaching snowsports requires more than just providing folks with information about their chosen sport and how to perform. Unlike coaching team sports, teachers in the mountain environment must cope with many external issues. The challenge of sliding on snow, the fear of falling or failing, and the concerns of just maintaining control make teaching snowsports a rewarding challenge.

Meaningful Relationships
The biggest factor in determining teaching successes or failures is the ability to relate successfully with students. Building meaningful relationships is key to establishing the trust required to overcome the challenges of learning a chosen sport. This manual points out the various criteria involved in relating with students and helps the teacher incorporate the uniqueness of his or her own personality in the process.

Unforgettable Experiences
Those who live the mountain lifestyle appreciate the experiences snowsports offer. Being immersed in the beauty of the mountains, sharing it with friends, and feeling the wind as you glide on the snow are unlike anything else. Proficiency at snowsports is a small, yet critical part of an experience that speaks to the human spirit. Many teachers have become best friends with their peers and students through the shared challenges and successes. This is an important added benefit of the job. The underlying purpose of this manual is to help teachers create unforgettable experiences for themselves and their students. The ultimate measure of the success of a snowsports teacher is the ability to make "once in a lifetime experiences" happen over and over again.

Successful Learning
Successful snowsports instructors measure their success by how proficient their students become. They also know that their students will learn more easily in an environment that is caring and comfortable, yet challenging. This manual will help the reader identify the barriers to learning and gain insight into how to remove them. By effectively managing the learning environment, a teacher has the power to facilitate learning.

- KNOWING YOURSELF
- DISCOVERING YOUR STUDENTS
- COACHING YOUR STUDENTS
- WORKING RELATIONSHIPS

Knowing Yourself

chapter 1

- WHY DO YOU WANT TO TEACH?

- BE HONEST WITH YOURSELF

- CONNECT WITH YOUR STUDENTS

- WHAT IS YOUR PICTURE OF SUCCESS?

- LEARN ABOUT YOURSELF

> *"You teach best what you most need to learn."*
> — RICHARD BACH
> ILLUSIONS: THE ADVENTURES OF A RELUCTANT MESSIAH

Why Do You Want to Teach?

The first step in being a successful teacher is to understand yourself and your motivations (photo 1.1). Why do you want to be a snowsports teacher, anyway? What draws you to it? Here's a list of some common reasons people get involved in teaching winter sports:

- I think it would be fun!
- My friends are doing it.
- I need a way to earn a living so I can stay in the mountains; I love this lifestyle!
- I've heard that the best way to learn more about something is to teach it.
- It would be cool to build a career in the resort industry.

These are all great reasons to get started, but you'll soon find many more. Whatever your reasons, success will come sooner if your top priority is to learn to build relationships with new people and to share yourself and your excitement for the sport.

Be Honest with Yourself

"Your conscience is the measure of the honesty of your selfishness. Listen to it carefully."
— BACH

Before giving yourself to a relationship, you must understand what you have to offer and need in return. Being honest with yourself about your own motivations and tendencies, your own strengths and weaknesses, is critical to an open and effective relationship with your students (fig. 1.1).

FIGURE 1.1 Anxiety is normal in unfamiliar situations.

It's almost my turn to teach. My palms are sweating. This is nerve-wracking! Will they like me? Will they learn? I've never taught before. What am I supposed to know about this? Is all this worry and nervousness worth it? Will I be good at it? Will it be fun? Meeting all those new people is a little overwhelming. Maybe I'm not good enough to do this.

PHOTO 1.1 What is *your* motivation to teach?

NATHAN BILOW

PHOTO 1.2 Take time to make a connection with each and every student.

BRIAN W. ROBB

Ultimately, your success as a teacher in any subject is dependent on your ability to connect on a personal level (photo 1.2). One of the best ways to see this connection in action is to think about your favorite teachers, coaches, or mentors. What were they like? Chances are, they were:

- Passionate about the sport or subject, and competent in it.
- Concerned for your experience and welfare.
- Confident in their abilities and your potential, yet open to new possibilities.
- Patient and persistent.
- Able to communicate in whatever way you needed.
- Willing to allow experiences and time to help them grow and learn.
- Able to function in multiple roles: coach, friend, guide, mentor, or student.

Recognizing the elements that combine to create your own personal style can help you to use these traits positively, avoid abusing them, and recognize them in others.

Connect with Your Students

"My ability to connect with my students and to connect them with the subject depends less on the methods I use than on the degree to which I know and trust my selfhood—and am willing to make it available and vulnerable in the service of learning."
— PARKER PALMER
   THE COURAGE TO TEACH

Imagine sharing yourself with a student. What does it feel like? What is your picture of success? Will you tell people what they need to know, or will you help them create what they want?

- **Interview with a Student Teacher #1** — "Welcome to Mt. Snows-a-Lot! We sure are glad you came! I know that you haven't tried this sport before, so I'm here to guide you every step of the way. You must be eager to get started, so let's not waste any more time. Now let's get out there and do it!"
- **Interview with a Student Teacher #2** — "Welcome to Mt. Snows-a-Lot! We sure are glad you came! I know that you must have some questions for me, and I sure have some for you, so let's get those out of the way before we hit the slopes. First, what made you decide to try this sport?"

"The power of our mentors is not necessarily in the models of good teaching they gave us, models that may turn out to have little to do with who we are as teachers. Their power is in their capacity to awaken a truth within us, a truth we can reclaim years later by recalling their impact on our lives. If we discovered a teacher's heart in ourselves by meeting a great teacher, recalling that meeting may help us take heart in teaching once more."
— PALMER

What is Your Picture of Success?

While following the example of a favorite mentor can help put you on the right track, you probably will gradually develop your own unique style as you learn more about yourself, your students, and the sport. Whatever model you choose, any veteran will tell you to be patient and keep your expectations realistic. It takes a while to get really good at this profession—like any other—but the successes and rewards can be found all along the way.

Learn about Yourself

"By reflecting upon your experiences, your learning, and your development as both a [participant] and instructor [or coach], you will uncover the most meaningful aspects of your role as a teacher: to instill in others the elation of discovery, the satisfaction of learning, and the love of [the sport]."
— PSIA Alpine Manual

The following chapters of this manual provide many opportunities to learn about yourself. You will gain insights into how you process and integrate new information, your own preferred learning style, your preferred method of interacting with others, and how you handle conflict. From this self-knowledge comes the realization that your natural style is not the only one—and that, while it works best for you, it won't work best for all of your students. Understanding and appreciating other styles will help you meet the needs of your students—and perhaps give you a fresh perspective on yourself.

Discovering Your Students

chapter 2

- MENTAL PROCESSES
- EMOTIONS AND LEARNING
- LEARNING TO MOVE

> *"You are never the main event.*
> *The real show is in your student's mind."*
> — Jensen
> Super Teaching

After your personal motivations, intentions, and tendencies are clear to you, it's time to focus on the other half of the relationship: your students. After all, you can't build a relationship with them if you don't know who they are. Even before asking basic questions about their wants or needs, it's important to understand a little bit about the body/mind connections wired into humans and how they affect the way people learn (fig. 2.1).

How people are put together, grow, develop, and process new information is highly variable. Gaining an appreciation for what makes your students tick in the following three areas—mental processes, emotions, and learning to move—will help you guide them successfully.

FIGURE 2.1 Proficiency Triad

Mental Processes
How does my brain work?

+

Emotional/ Social Development
What affects my attitude towards learning?

+

Physical Capacity
What is my body capable of?

Mental Processes

"The growth of the human mind is still high adventure, in many ways the highest adventure on earth."
— Norman Cousins
quoted in Hannaford
Smart Moves

Understanding how people process information is critical to understanding how they learn, and therefore how best to teach them.

HOW THE BRAIN WORKS

From infancy onward, every interaction with the world results in learning. Learning begins as specialized nerve cells, called neurons, make connections with other neurons in response to movement or sensory input. Groups of neurons build pathways that form a sort of map for the body to access information and react appropriately. As learning continues, these pathways form complex networks through which information is transmitted ever more quickly. The networks grow and change shape as new information creates new pathways.

When we first learn something, it goes slowly, like traveling a rough road. As the nerve cells are stimulated again and again, a fatty substance called myelin is laid down. Myelin, like blacktop on a road, smoothes the neural connections. More stimulation—movement, thought, memory—produces more myelin, and the pathway gets faster and faster, like driving on a super highway. This is the essence of "practice makes perfect."

Roy was an older gentleman who was learning to ski later in life. His preference was for personal coaching and his goal was to explore as much of the mountain in as many conditions as possible. Having fallen in love with skiing after his first try, he had introduced his whole family to the sport, bought a second home in the mountains, and was getting ready to take vacation time to explore different mountains.

On a crystal-clear, blue-sky morning, Roy was greeted by his instructor, Celia. Roy shook Celia's hand warmly and said, "Okay, kid, today I learn to carve. Don't worry about boring me, stopping me, or any of that. I learned early on from my golf coach that to really get something, you have to practice it over and over again. And if you really want to get better, you need a coach to watch and tell you if you're getting it. I don't frustrate easily, unless my coach isn't giving me the real stuff. So, are you ready?"

Boy, was Celia ready! But it's almost never that easy. The next day Celia coached a novice teenager who wanted to be the next Tomba. He could barely get down a green run, let alone do it with speed or style. Celia's challenge was to figure out how to get him to practice the right moves without boring or frustrating him.

SENSORY CONTRIBUTION

"Learning [consists of] changes in behavior resulting from human interactions or contacts with the environment. Learning occurs as a natural byproduct of living."
— KOLESNIK
  LEARNING: EDUCATIONAL
  APPLICATIONS

Learning is dependent on the sensori-motor systems through which all experiences are processed. Sensory information related to movement comes primarily through the visual, auditory, and kinesthetic (feeling and balance) senses. The way the brain processes this information is called the perceptual motor system. As we grow and develop, thought processes and emotions that help us learn are triggered through sensory stimulation.

"Real things happen when we experience with our senses, and in the experiencing we observe, relate to past experience, and notice patterns. Words are useful in this process; they help us organize our thoughts about the sensations. But they are no substitute for the force and vividness of actual experience."
— HANNAFORD

Not only are the senses the most important information gatherers when learning a motor sport, they also provide the entertainment—the fun or thrill—that draws most students to the sport in the first place.

Vision
The ability to perceive objects in terms of relative size, shape, distance, and position is critical for successful movement through space. Visual development is usually complete by age 7, but younger students may not be able to "see" clearly despite their visual acuity. While their vision may be sharp, their ability to process and interpret visual input is still developing. Understanding new or complex images may take a little longer for children, especially when they are excited about the new experience.

Visual acuity usually begins to decline in the 40s or 50s. With increasing age, most of us will eventually suffer declines in depth perception, peripheral vision, adaptation to light, ability to focus closely, tolerance to glare, and ability to distinguish colors. Keep this in mind when using visual cues to teach seniors.

Sounds
The ability to focus on one sound among many and determine where sounds are coming from is important when listening to someone and interpreting how to move relative to other people. For most people, the sense of hearing is perfect at birth and

gradually deteriorates through life. Young children may often seem as though they are "tuned out" when in reality they are "tuned in" to too many sounds. Refocusing their attention when giving verbal instructions to younger students can help them hear what you're saying.

After about age 50, most adults gradually lose the ability to discriminate certain sounds, and older individuals may have difficulty separating your voice from background noise. As with vision, declining auditory acuity needs to be taken into account when dealing with seniors.

Sense of Motion

One of the first sensory systems to fully develop is the vestibular system, which controls balance and the sense of movement. Located in the inner ear, the vestibular system provides information about the position of the head relative to the ground. These sensory organs are among the most sensitive in the body—a good thing, because they keep our head in the right orientation, whether we are moving or stationary!

Intimately tied with the vestibular system is the proprioceptive system. This system gives us our sense of where we are in space—another key element in sliding down a mountain. Proprioceptors in each muscle fiber monitor the amount of flexion or extension. The brain uses this information to maintain balance and alignment during motion, ranging from keeping our eyes steady while reading to adjusting our body position as we navigate through bumps.

Feeling or Touch

Kinesthetic awareness is the ability to perceive body positions through feeling or touch. The ability to feel the snow sliding beneath your feet and distinguish differing amounts of force or friction is important for learning to adjust and refine movements.

TABLE 2.1 Piaget's Stages of Development

Stage	Things You Might Hear
SENSORIMOTOR—BIRTH TO AGE 2 Characteristics Explore the world through sensory stimuli.	"Oooooh! Snow is cold!" "I'm hungry."
PRE-OPERATIONS—AGE 2 TO 6 Characteristics Understanding based on prior experience or sensory input. Unable to manipulate objects in space mentally. Think in terms of "what is."	"Why is it called a 'gator' [gaiter]?" "That turn was louder than the last kind we tried." "Which is my right side?"
CONCRETE OPERATIONS—AGE 6 TO 10 Characteristics Thinking mostly based on concrete objects, but beginning to visualize and manipulate objects mentally. Can imagine "what if."	"I want to go back to the the first run and stop by those big trees on the right." "If I don't turn so far, won't I go too fast and fall down?"
FORMAL OPERATIONS—AGE 10+ Characteristics Abstract thinking is beginning to develop. Concepts or ideals such as "fairness" and "responsibility" now have meaning.	"I like it here, but I guess it would be good to try a different trail, and it's Susie's turn to choose." "Those guys shouldn't go under that rope. The trail's closed."

The sense of touch can have another use in teaching. A reassuring—but appropriate—touch can help create a sense of caring, allay fear, or reinforce other sensory input. Be careful to avoid touching that is intrusive, unwelcome, or open to misinterpretation by the person being touched or others in the group.

DEVELOPMENT OF MENTAL PROCESSES

"People learn from many different sources, in many ways, and at various rates.... Individuals respond differently to similar stimuli. Our learning patterns are more like a three-dimensional, geometric expansion, rather than a straight-lined, arithmetical progression."
— Horst Abraham
   Skiing Right

Experiences create the connections in the brain that produce memory, thought, and understanding. Young children don't understand information in the same way as adults.

Further, the way an individual understands is largely influenced by past experiences that have shaped the way new information is received and processed.

Jean Piaget, who observed children and categorized what he saw into stages of development, has provided a relatively simple way of understanding changes in brain function as children grow. Everyone passes through these stages in order, yet what is considered the "normal" age for each may vary (table 2.1).

While somewhat simplistic—and challenged by some modern researchers—Piaget's empirical (observation-based) classification dovetails nicely with what is known about the physical development of the brain. For those interested in this topic, Hannaford (1995) delves into this topic in detail, including information on the influence of hormones beginning with adolescence and the continued development and refinement of the higher brain until approximately age 30.

What happens to mental processing during the later years of life? Among other changes are slower responses to terrain, speed, light, and other variables. Awareness of these factors is critical when teaching seniors.

In short, it is important to understand the developmental capabilities of any student so that your expectations for performance, understanding, and communication are reasonable and appropriate for their developmental stage. This awareness can save the learner and the teacher needless frustration and provide freedom to explore what is possible.

LEARNING STYLES AND PREFERENCES

"Learning is finding out what you already know. Doing is demonstrating that you know it. Teaching is reminding others that they know just as well as you. You are all learners, doers, teachers."
— BACH

An individual's preferred learning style is determined by how she or he receives, processes, and absorbs information. Teachers can use the awareness of different learning styles to help choose the best teaching strategies for individuals, or combination of strategies to cover the different styles within a group (fig. 2.2).

In reality, no single learning style is appropriate for any one person.

Instead, an individual may use many styles depending on the circumstances surrounding the learning environment. Jensen (1995) divides the learning process into four categories:

- **Readiness**—The circumstances surrounding the learning situation—physical, environmental, social, emotional.
- **Reception**—The preferred sensory input mode for the individual learner (visual, auditory, kinesthetic).
- **Processing**—The method of digesting and absorbing information—brain hemisphere dominance, etc.
- **Reaction**—What the individual does with the information.

In 1971, research by David Kolb on learning style preferences generated much discussion among educators. The result was an extensive study by The National Association of Secondary School Principals, which concluded that learning styles are "the composite of characteristic cognitive, affective, and physiological factors that serve as relatively stable indicators of how a learner perceives, interacts with, and responds to the learning environment."

Kolb's work provides a simple approach to learning styles. He separates learning into two different aspects: perception and processing (table 2.2).

TABLE 2.2 Perception and Processing

Perception
- Big Picture/Feeler
- Parts/Thinker

Processing
- Active Experimenters: Doers
- Reflective Observers: Watchers

- **Perception** is the way a person views the world and collects the information to be learned. On either end of the perception continuum are two types of learners: "big picture" learners (or "feelers" as Abraham has called them) and "parts" learners (or "thinkers").
- **Processing** is how we mentally manipulate the information in a way to help us learn it. At either end of the processing continuum are "reflective observers" ("watchers") and "active experimenters" ("doers").

A number of learning theorists have researched and refined Kolb's four basic types of learners. Bernice McCarthy (About Learning, Inc.) developed the 4MAT system of instruction based on Kolb's work (fig. 2.3). McCarthy's classification scheme may be summarized as follows:

- **Type 1 —"innovative learners"** See the whole first, then the parts. Sense the world and reflect on it before making decisions about learning. Often very sensitive and creative. Respond to and trust their emotions. Good at sharing and learn best in discussions. Place emphasis on making sense of the world is important. Favorite question is "why."
- **Type 2 —"analytical learners"** Quiet observers. Perceive details first, then develop an understanding of the whole. Analytical and studious. Organized, detailed, accurate, and patient. Want to

FIGURE 2.2 The Learning Process

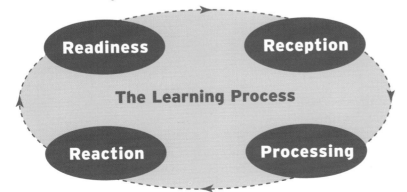

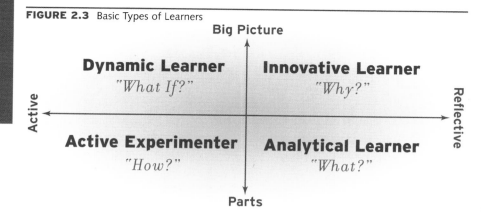

FIGURE 2.3 Basic Types of Learners

Big Picture

Active — **Reflective**

Dynamic Learner
"What If?"

Innovative Learner
"Why?"

Active Experimenter
"How?"

Analytical Learner
"What?"

Parts

know "what" needs to be accomplished and set a deliberate path toward the solution.

- **Type 3—"active experimenters"** Also proceed from details to the whole but learn best when actively engaged in manipulating and using the concept in the environment. Very pragmatic and practical problem solvers. Active processing style is prone to both creativity and errors. Favorite questions concern "how" things work and how they can be used to solve problems.

- **Type 4—"dynamic learners"** Sensory. Proceed from the whole to the parts but are also active processors and need to be actively engaged in a learning situation. "People person" learners. Shape reality as they try to determine "what if" an idea, skill, or tool is used in a particular manner. Tend to jump right into a situation and try intuitive (gut) solutions to problems. Though sometimes seen as a lack of discipline, this is actually their brand of discipline at work."

In real life, of course, very few people fall into such tidy categories. While understanding these categories can provide some insights into learning styles, it is best to assume that your students are more complex. Indeed, most people learn by a combination of two or three styles, depending on the material, the learning environment, and the particular day (or even the time of day!).

How can you deal with such complexity? The best way is to provide a rich, multisensory learning experience that addresses all four types of learning. Since most teachers present information in their own preferred learning mode, using a more varied approach requires awareness and focus.

MULTIPLE INTELLIGENCES

"In these fertile encounters with an object or a situation, one discovers that one possesses a hitherto unsuspected combination of intelligences, and proceeds to develop that strand of talent. Such encounters occur with ordinary individuals, as when a youngster discovers a special gift at chess or bowling, as well as with the gifted, as when young Einstein's receipt of a compass stimulated his thinking about physical forces."

— HOWARD GARDNER
FRAMES OF MIND

One of the most important things you can discover about your students is that all are gifted in one way or another. Each brings a wealth of unique experiences and proficiencies when venturing into the world of snowsports. This ranges from a child who knows how to skate or sing a silly song to an adult who knows how to drive a car or plays basketball in a

community league. Some of these proficiencies will naturally help them learn snowsports; others will require a more creative approach for making a connection.

Howard Gardner (1985) described the theory of multiple intelligences, blowing apart traditional thinking about the validity of IQ and intelligence as it had previously been defined. Gardner postulated that intelligence is really the ability to use a skill, create something of value to society, or solve a problem in a way that is valued by a particular culture. Gardner describes seven categories of intelligence:

1. **Verbal-Linguistic**
   Characterized by a love of words and language, reading and talking, or telling and listening to stories (word-smart).

2. **Logical-Mathematical**
   Characterized by someone who asks "why" and "how," recognizes patterns easily, follows logical steps or creates them, and works to solve problems (logic- or numbers-smart).

3. **Spatial**
   Characterized by someone who has an active imagination, is adept at manipulating shapes and objects in space (including self) and sensitive to the balance and organization of those shapes, and who likes to design, draw, organize, and do puzzles (picture-smart).

4. **Bodily-Kinesthetic**
   Characterized by a desire to move and an ability to move skillfully, including moving objects skillfully for art or function; this person is often seen touching or manipulating something (e.g., hair or clothing) and seems to be in perpetual motion (body-smart).

5. **Musical-Rhythmic**
   Characterized by a propensity for sounds and rhythm and making music; this person is often heard

humming, singing, or tapping to make rhythm (music-smart).

6. **Interpersonal**
   Characterized by someone who is adept in social situations, discerns the emotional states of others and responds appropriately, and is persuasive as a negotiator or leader (people-smart).

7. **Intrapersonal**
   Characterized by someone who likes solitude, thinks a lot, likes to work alone, understands personal strengths and weaknesses, and easily sets personal goals (self-smart).

Further complicating these categories of intelligence is the fact that the profile for an individual is not static for a lifetime. In fact, the profile may dramatically change depending on what Gardner calls "crystallizing experiences."

Each of these areas has relevance in snowsports. Some may be challenging to a teacher who is proficient in different areas from the students. The key is to understand that these areas exist and, rather than being thwarted by them, use them to reach your students.

"How smart are you?" is now irrelevant... a more powerful new question is, "How are you smart?"
— JENSEN

Emotions and Learning

"As we experience the world, the collage of images and our responding actions are all run through an emotional filter...that determines the value, meaning, and survival potential of the experience in light of past experience"
— HANNAFORD

Your ability to bring the emotions of your students into the learning environment may be the linchpin for a

successful learning experience. Enthusiasts describe snowsports participation with almost reverent, spiritual images. Yet, past efforts at describing the learning process for winter sport teachers has emphasized the technical components of the sport and methods for teaching it, failing to recognize the potential of teaching for emotional involvement.

Emotion can be a powerful component in creating long-term memory of an event—and hence learning (photo 2.1). Each new experience is given its value and meaning based on its relationship to past experiences, filtered through the kaleidoscope of emotion. When our brain perceives an experience as a threat, adrenaline is released, inhibiting the ability to process other information. Learning is almost impossible for a student who is scared, until the cause of the fear is removed and the body's chemistry returns to normal.

EMOTIONAL AND SOCIAL DEVELOPMENT

As with the development of senses, we must develop emotions through exploration of social experiences and practicing emotional expression. At around 15 months of age, we begin to take notice of others and interact socially. By age 2, we realize that we are separate beings and can have a place and things of our own. "Mine!" is a typical 2-year-old exclamation. This recognition is the beginning of finding our sense of self, ultimately defined by our relationships with others.

Also at about age 2, we begin to fully practice the expression of emotions. Anyone who has ever witnessed the temper tantrum of a 2-year-old knows this well. During the tantrum,

The Spirit of Skiing
When the cold autumn winds blow,
A fire deep within me is rekindled.
With winter's first flurries,
This passion remembered starts
     to burn.
Skimming o'er the frozen white,
Leaving life's ails behind in a cloud
     of icy smoke.
I'm free for a moment in time, free.
I dance the dance called skiing.
I fly this wingless flight.
Sensations abound, nourishing and
Vitalizing my body and spirit.
I ride the wind. I fly. I ski.
It is a dialogue, a colloquy.
On the white canvas I paint and etch
     my every mood.
The shiny slope mirrors and
     I know myself better.
I share this passion with those I meet.
I give this gift, I pass on joy.
Hail skiing, hail teaching,
     hail ski teaching.
I love it so, for it makes me who I am.
I ride the wind, I fly, I ski.
— DAVE MERRIAM
   PSIA-AASI NATIONAL
   DEMONSTRATION TEAMS COACH

the child is consumed by the emotion and cannot separate the behavior from the feeling.

As we continue to develop—and as instinctive emotions become better integrated with thought—more sophisticated emotions emerge. So too does the ability to control behaviors in socially acceptable ways. Mercifully, this development occurs by approximately 4 years of age. Even then, the emotions remain "raw," and the little person is still very much controlled by the feelings.

Continued brain development is also evidenced when a child begins to develop relationships with others. Typically, children from age 3 to about age 6 learn to develop key relationships with adults. The main goal is to please the adults in their world and do as the adults model. This changes at about age 7, as children begin to question authority and try to prove that they are smarter. This is also a way of distinguishing and defining the self.

In adolescent years, the social norms of one's subculture or group become more important than those of authority figures. This association is driven by the need to find an identity and gain the acceptance of a chosen social group.

Finally, in adulthood, we associate what is good and bad with individual values such as justice and dignity. Yet, even as adults we never reach the stage where individual autonomy totally rules our thinking. We are wired for survival, which usually includes harmony within the clan. This instinctive need is evidenced by our willingness to "go with the flow" in so many situations where our individual preference may differ.

PHOTO 2.1 We remember experiences tied to powerful images, emotions, and values.

BRIAN W. ROBB

PLAY

Through make-believe and pretend, children learn to express emotion, play roles, and build relationships. As the play progresses, neural connections are made that develop the base patterns on which future experiences will be integrated.

As babies, play focuses on sensory experience. Infants interact with whatever is in their grasp or sight. As toddlers, they begin to notice the existence of other children and may play side by side, but without interacting. Only if one child's impulse is thwarted by another will any significant interaction occur, and only then to express anger or frustration.

By age 3, children begin interacting and playing free-form "let's pretend" games that evolve as the children

desire. The games have a simple context, such as "house," and it all flows from there. By about age 4 or 5, games with rules and rituals are introduced, but it isn't until about age 7 or 8 that the games have real winners, losers, and formalized results such as scores. At this age, children begin noticing improvement and become motivated by outcomes and results.

MEMORY

Try to remember as far back in your life as you can. Your early memories are apt to be powerful ones, rich with smells, sounds, textures, and emotions. Early memories help us define our experiences in context. For example, we become able to describe food—originally only a requisite for survival—as being fun to eat, fun to play with, colored like mom's shirt, squishy, cold, etc.

For development of a rich and full memory, emotional value and meaning must be attached. Studies have shown that the ability to recall lists of words is greater when the words evoke powerful images and emotions (table 2.3).

TABLE 2.3 Memory Drill	
The	Powder
And	Epic
That	Carve
What	Snowstorm

Your brain has undoubtedly attached powerful images, emotion, and value to the second list (if you are a mountain-lover!). The first list, even though containing simpler words, has no emotional content or context and will probably be more difficult to remember. Memory is a random-access system that uses emotional cues to retrieve information from all areas of the brain simultaneously. Successful learning is more likely if the experience is connected to a meaningful sensory, physical, or emotional episode. The more of these experiences we encounter, the easier it becomes to integrate the new information with the base pattern.

SUMMARY – EMOTIONS AND LEARNING

The "moral of the story" is that making a learning experience emotionally charged will cause your students to view it as more valuable and meaningful. It is the sense of value and meaning that brings us all back to the mountains.

- What was your most powerful learning experience?
- Do you remember sights and sounds clearly?
- Do you remember words or actions from your coach?
- Could you relate the story? What made it valuable for you?
- What emotion do you feel as you relive the experience?
- What can you take from that experience into your own coaching?

Learning to Move

"An understanding of anatomy (the body's structure) links the concepts of mechanics to human motion. Movement principles and body structure determine both the possibilities and limitations in movement."
— PSIA ALPINE MANUAL

The two aspects of human anatomy most relevant to teaching snowsports are biomechanics (how the body moves) and physical development (how the body grows and changes with age). Understanding how people move and what they are capable of at different ages and stages will help keep expectations realistic as you facilitate and guide the learning process.

Diana was standing at the bottom of the short pitch. She could see her group of students—a family she had been coaching for a couple of days—assembling at the top. They were awaiting her signal for each to descend toward the waiting camera. As she waved the first performer on, Diana began to notice how differently they all moved. From dad, to mom, to the 12-year-old boy, right to the 6-year-old daughter, each had a distinctive way of moving. Diana knew that she had to coach them each in different ways, but what could they really do? What were the limitations, and what were the opportunities?

ANATOMY 101

To teach effectively, it is important to understand the capabilities of the human body relative to movement. The musculoskeletal system, which is responsible for movement, consists of muscles, bones, connective tissues, and joints.

Muscles
Muscles do the physical work of the human system. A muscle can either contract or relax. Contractions can be concentric, eccentric, and isometric.
- **Concentric Contraction**—when a muscle performs work by getting shorter (e.g., using the biceps to lift a weight by bending the elbow).
- **Eccentric Contraction**—when a muscle performs work while getting longer (e.g., using the biceps to lower your favorite after-sport beverage by straightening the elbow).
- **Isometric Contraction**—when a muscle performs work while staying the same length (e.g., when body builders tense their muscles while holding a pose).

We unconsciously use isometric contractions to stabilize the joints and maintain balance. This is one reason why most new snowsports participants get so tired on their first day. (The other is the energy required to get back on their feet after plentiful contact with the snow!)

Connective Tissues
Tissues that hold muscles and bones together include cartilage, ligaments, and tendons. Cartilage provides a cushion between bones in a joint. Ligaments connect bones in a joint. The tightness of the ligaments determines the range of motion and stability of the joint. Tendons connect muscle to bone and create movements of the joints by transferring forces from muscle to bone.

FIGURE 2.4 The Skeleton and Major Types of Joints

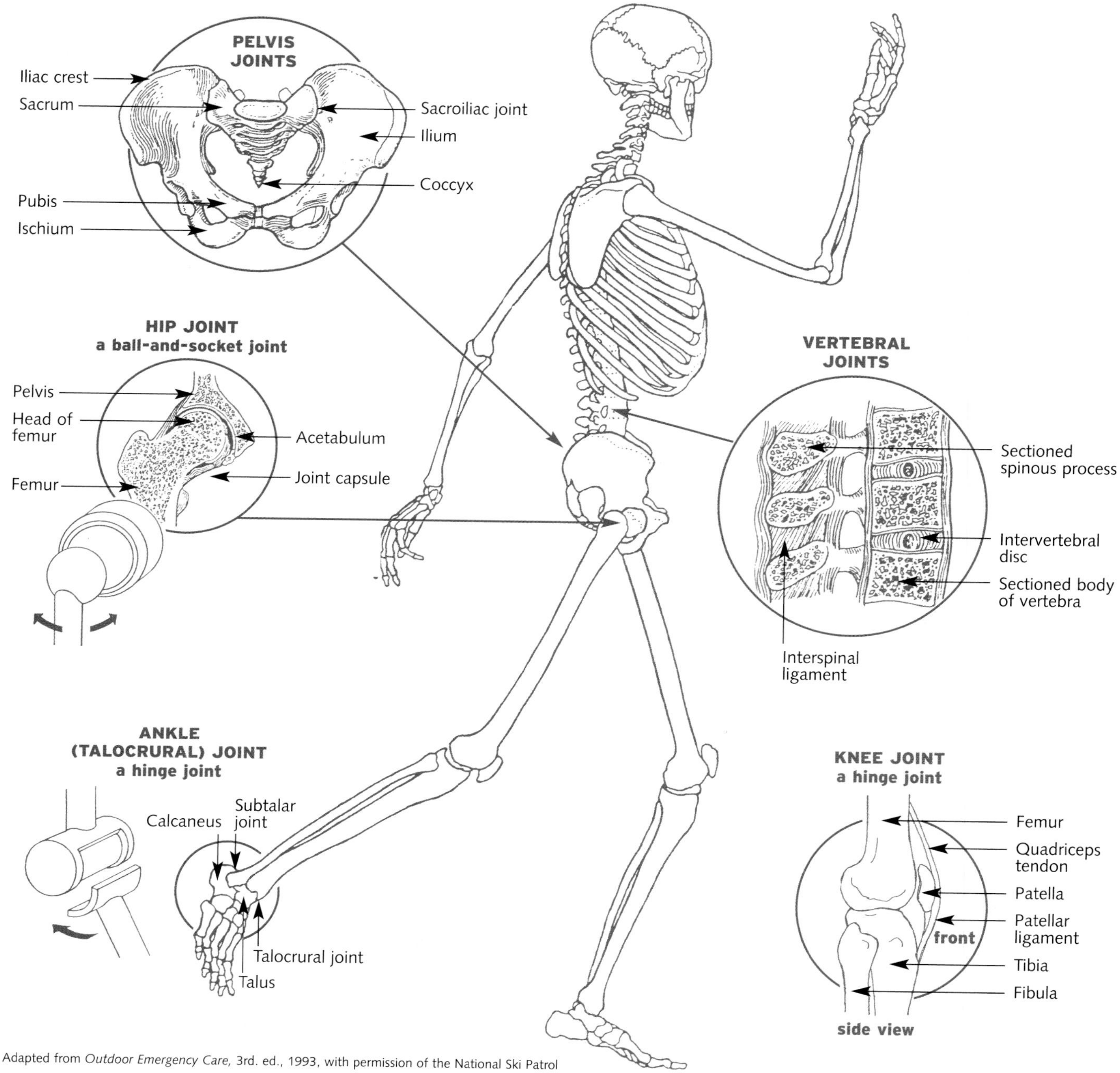

PELVIS JOINTS
Iliac crest
Sacrum
Sacroiliac joint
Ilium
Coccyx
Pubis
Ischium

HIP JOINT
a ball-and-socket joint
Pelvis
Head of femur
Acetabulum
Femur
Joint capsule

VERTEBRAL JOINTS
Sectioned spinous process
Intervertebral disc
Sectioned body of vertebra
Interspinal ligament

ANKLE (TALOCRURAL) JOINT
a hinge joint
Subtalar joint
Calcaneus
Talocrural joint
Talus

KNEE JOINT
a hinge joint
Femur
Quadriceps tendon
Patella
Patellar ligament
front
Tibia
Fibula
side view

Adapted from *Outdoor Emergency Care*, 3rd. ed., 1993, with permission of the National Ski Patrol

Bones and Joints

Bones are the strongest tissue in the body and provide the structure that supports muscles and other tissues. In terms of movement, bones are the levers that the muscles use to transmit and amplify power (fig. 2.4).

Every bone-to-bone connection in the body occurs at a joint. The joints of primary interest to snowsports enthusiasts are the ankle, knee, hip, and spine. The movement possibilities at each joint depend on the structural relationship of the muscle, bone, and connective tissue.

What we loosely call the ankle actually includes two joints: The subtalar joint connects the talus (the bone below the shin bone, or tibia) with the calcaneus (heel bone) and is responsible for foot rotation.

This rotation can be either inward (inversion) or outward (eversion). The talocrural joint connects the bones of the lower leg (the tibia and fibula) to the talus. This hinge-type joint is responsible for flexion and extension of the ankle. Ankle flexion is a movement of the toes toward the shin. Ankle extension is a movement of the toes away from the shin (fig. 2.5).

FIGURE 2.5 Directions of Foot Movement

Dorsiflexion   Plantar flexion   Inversion   Eversion

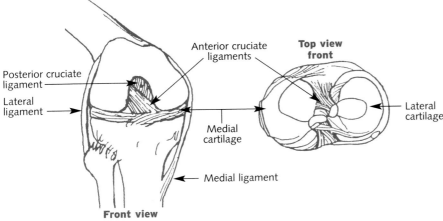

Reprinted from *Alpine Manual* (PSIA 1996)

FIGURE 2.6 Knee Joint and Ligaments

Posterior cruciate ligament

Lateral ligament

Anterior cruciate ligaments

Top view front

Lateral cartilage

Medial cartilage

Medial ligament

Front view

Reprinted from *Outdoor Emergency Care*, 3rd ed., 1993, with permission of the National Ski Patrol

PHOTO 2.2 Gravity Rules!

FIGURE 2.7 The center of mass moves through a turn.

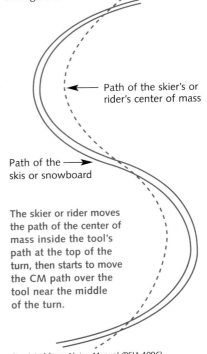

Path of the skier's or rider's center of mass

Path of the skis or snowboard

The skier or rider moves the path of the center of mass inside the tool's path at the top of the turn, then starts to move the CM path over the tool near the middle of the turn.

Reprinted from *Alpine Manual* (PSIA 1996)

The knee, which connects the thigh bone (femur) with the shin (tibia), is also a hinge joint. The knee cap (patella) covers and protects the knee joint. As with other hinge-type joints, the knee is capable of only fore-and-aft movements. Flexion is bending the knee, and extension is straightening the knee.

Five ligaments help stabilize the knee. The medial collateral ligament (MCL) stabilizes the side of the knee adjacent to the other leg, while the lateral collateral ligament (LCL) stabilizes the outer side of the knee. The infamous anterior cruciate ligament (ACL) prevents forward movement of the tibia relative to the femur, while the posterior cruciate ligament (PCL) prevents backward movement. The patellar ligament connects the patella to the tibia and is an extension of the patellar tendon (fig. 2.6).

The femur and pelvis meet at the hip joint. The hip is a ball-and-socket joint, which is more stable than a hinge joint and allows movement in all directions (the shoulder is another ball-and-socket joint). The hip joint allows three pairs of movements of the femur: flexion/extension (lifting/ lowering), abduction/adduction (opening/closing), and medial/lateral rotation (inward/ outward).

The spine comprises 33 separate bones called vertebrae, some of which are fused together. The spine allows the following three types of movement: flexion/extension, lateral flexion, and rotation. All of these are used in snowsports.

PHYSICS

Understanding basic laws of physics can help you predict and manage the behavior of snow tools (photo 2.2). Sir Isaac Newton described three laws

that affect all types of motion:

1. A body in motion will remain in motion until acted upon by a force, and a body at rest will remain at rest until acted upon by a force.
2. Two masses are attracted toward each other.
3. For every action is an equal and opposite reaction. We push on the snow and the snow pushes back.

Gravity is the attraction of two masses toward each other—in our sports, gravity is what propels us down a slope. The center of mass (CM), also known as the center of gravity, is the average position of the mass of an object in three dimensions: front-back (sagittal axis), left-right (frontal axis), and up-down (vertical or longitudinal axis). When humans stand erect, the CM is near the navel. When analyzing how forces such as gravity act on the body, picture the forces being applied at the CM (fig. 2.7).

Momentum or inertia is the tendency to remain in motion or at rest, unless acted upon by a force. Momentum is calculated by multiplying the mass of an object by its velocity. The faster an object moves, or the greater its mass, the greater its momentum.

In snowsports, another important aspect of physics is referred to as the tangent—defined as the direction a snow tool (and its human user!) would follow if it were to suddenly break away from a turn. The tangent of a curve is oriented perpendicular to the radius of the curve at that point. In maintaining a turn, a participant must constantly overcome the tendency of the snow tool to go in the direction of the tangent instead of continuing to follow along the circumference (arc) of the turn. The strength of the tendency to break away from a turn is related to speed, mass, and the radius of curvature.

PHYSICAL GROWTH AND DEVELOPMENT

An awareness of physical development will help explain why and how people move. This awareness will enable you to understand both the possibilities and limits of physical movement as you create real and attainable goals for your students, no matter what age or level.

After watching "her" family through the lens of the video camera, Diana realized that she would need to be especially discerning in her descriptions of each, because they exhibited, and were capable of, very different levels of performance. In addition, any inadvertent words on the tape could crush an unsuspecting psyche. But what were the true differences? Where were Diana's opportunities for coaching, and where were her expectations off the mark?

Basic Developmental Principles
Studying the silhouette of a 5-year-old next to a 25-year-old would show some obvious differences—not just in size, but in their body shape and proportion, how they stand and balance, and how they use their arms and legs. While physical development occurs in a predictable sequence, the rate of maturation of each component varies from person to person. Three major aspects of physical growth that pertain to snowsports involve muscular development, changes in the CM, and increased coordination.

Muscular Development
Development of the muscular system as humans grow from infants to children to adolescents proceeds as follows:
- from head to feet
- from the center of the body to the extremities
- from gross to fine motor control

This can readily be seen when comparing young skiers or snowboarders to adults. Children tend to move as a relatively rigid unit, while adults are able to move different parts of the body independently—e.g., the upper half relative to the lower half, and the right half relative to the left half.

Changes in the Center of Mass
Changes in the CM during growth are related primarily to the disproportionately large head of a child compared to an adult. This causes a child's CM to be located slightly higher in the torso. Since balance is achieved by keeping the CM over the base of support when stationary, or slightly ahead of it while sliding downslope, a relatively small change in head position of a child can have a bigger impact on stability than with an adult. This is exacerbated by the fact that muscles used to control balance are not as well developed.

Coordination
The development of coordination is another component of physical maturation. Coordination is related to physical development but also relies on practice and experience. When learning new movements, people move through three basic stages of development, which are lengthened for someone who has not yet matured. These are called the initial, elementary, and mature stages.

1. **Initial Stage**
   The student shows total unfamiliarity with the movement and relies on sensory information and coaching for learning it. The student typically seeks visual feedback by looking at whatever body part is involved.
2. **Elementary Stage**
   The student can perform the movement without looking at the involved part of the body but still needs to think it through and concentrate on the parts.
3. **Mature Stage**
   The student can perform the movement fluidly and automatically, without conscious thought. Reaching this stage often requires more time and practice than students and/or teachers expect.

Keola was exasperated: "I feel like a total klutz; it's useless."

"Do you do other sports?" asked Stasia, his instructor.

"Well," Keola replied, "I ride my mountain bike all over the Big Island."

"Think back," Stasia said, "do you remember the first time you ever rode a bike as a kid? Did it come easily, or did you have to concentrate on the handlebar, the pedals, and your balance? I'll bet you didn't do much looking around."

Keola thought for a moment, then laughed: "I guess it was pretty difficult, and I did fall a few times. I really had to focus on staying on the bike. Of course, it's all automatic now, just like surfing."

"Same thing with this sport," Stasia reassured him. "You're having to learn a whole new way of moving. Just keep working at it, and you'll get to where this feels totally comfortable and natural—just like riding that bike."

THE AGING PROCESS

"There is no defining aging/elderly; you are as young as you think, and 'keeping it moving' makes you feel better and better!"

— Gwen Allard
 PSIA–AASI Adaptive
 Committee Chair

Bone Mass

In men, testosterone stimulates bone (and muscle) growth, enabling men to enter the second half of their lives with ample bone reserves. Bone density in men eventually begins to decline with age, but usually not until the 70s or 80s. The situation is much different for women, who add bone mass only until about age 30. Bone density is then maintained until the mid-30s but begins gradually to decline— becoming more rapid with the onset of menopause.

Some recent research indicates that bone loss in women can be slowed or prevented to some extent by exercise and dietary supplements.

Muscle Mass and Strength

Most people attain maximum muscle strength in the mid-20s to mid-30s. By the 40s, muscle strength begins to decrease, especially in the lower body, due to loss of muscle mass. This loss can be substantially reduced by exercise.

Muscle Endurance

Endurance is measured as the length of time an individual can hold a certain percentage of his or her maximal force until fatigue or as the number of times an individual an repeatedly lift a percentage of maximal weight. Age-related declines in endurance are less than declines in strength. For example, aging runners experience less of a decrease in performance at longer distances, where stamina is the key.

Motor Performance

"Motor performance, the execution of tasks that require coordinated muscle activity, is of primary concern to aging adults because it is the basis for activities of daily living… job-related tasks, sports, and recreational pursuits. Each person is born a unique individual, and interaction of aging and life experiences increases the intra-individual and inter-individual variability in many variables across the life span. Therefore, descriptions of 'average' behavior for specific age groups grow less and less accurate for an individual's performance as the age of the group increases. Physiological changes occur with age, and these changes eventually limit motor performances. However, it is difficult to distinguish physiological changes due to aging per se from those due to declining physical activity, decreases in motivation, lower societal expectations, and the occurrence of disease."

— Spirduso and MacRae
 in Handbook of Psychology
 of Aging

Summary—Aging

To sum it up, exercise—including participation in snowsports—can be of great benefit to people as they age by helping them maintain physical strength and endurance. Exercise also appears to benefit some types of mental function, perhaps by improving the flow of blood and oxygen to the brain. The more active and fit your older students are, the longer they will be able to continue learning and enjoying the mountain environment.

"With practice and keeping physically fit, older people are able to 'stay in the game of life' and participate with/among people of younger years until disease or death take their toll!"

— Gwen Allard

GENDER DIFFERENCES

Some physical attributes affect how women learn snowsports. Strength is by far the largest gender difference affecting performance. Greater muscle mass allows men to apply and withstand greater force. To compensate, women often substitute precision and finesse. Other physical differences also affect performance:

- Women tend to have a lower CM because of the general "pear shape" of the typical female body. Men usually have wider shoulders and carry more weight above the waist. A lower CM may affect balancing when combined with lack of flexibility in the ankles by causing the weight to be shifted behind the base of support. While the generalized shape of a female body can exacerbate this problem, it is neither an issue with all women nor confined to women.

- The average woman has a wider pelvis, which puts the upper leg bone (femur) at a greater angle to the vertical. This is called the "Q angle" (fig. 2.8). A pronounced Q angle—recognized by someone who appears knock-kneed-affects edging for skiers (shims in boots can help compensate for this).

- Women have greater mobility in the hip socket than men (fig. 2.9). Greater flexibility requires more strength to control and stabilize the body. Given this mobility, female students may tend to use too much hip rotation when turning.

For more information, see Carbone (*Women Ski*) and Loring (*Skiing: A Woman's Guide*).

SUMMARY – LEARNING TO MOVE

- Learning is truly a function of the mind-body connection. Emotion is a key link to learning. Experiences that have deeper

---

FIGURE 2.8 The Q Angle

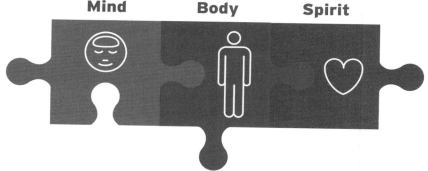

In general, the female pelvis is wider and shallower than the male pelvis, causing the femur to be at a greater angle between the pelvis and the knee. This position is called the "Q" angle.

Reprinted from *The Professional Skier* (PSIA, Fall 1993)

FIGURE 2.9 Hip Mobility

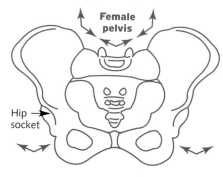
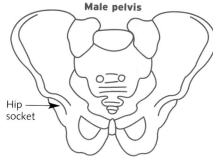

Movement of the pelvis relates to twisting the torso and the upper musculature of the body. Movement of the femur in the hip socket relates to pushing through the musculature of the leg and the pelvis.

Reprinted from *The Professional Skier* (PSIA, Fall 1993)

FIGURE 2.10 Learning engages the mind, body, and spirit.

Mind   Body   Spirit

---

meaning through emotion are more strongly remembered and more easily accessed.

- Students are gifted in different ways. It is up to the teacher to present new information using multiple approaches that address the differences.

- Human anatomy, combined with physical external forces, determines the limits and possibilities of movements. Age and gender differences also contribute to both limits and possibilities.

To be successful, remember to address the needs of the whole person (fig. 2.10). Mental, social/emotional, and physical parameters interact to create the learning capabilities of any student. With experience, teachers learn to recognize the gifts and talents their students bring to the learning environment and use these to facilitate deeper, meaningful experiences that hold value for both learner and teacher.

Coaching Your Students

chapter 3

- DEVELOPING TRUST

- ASSESSING MOVEMENTS

- WORKING THE LEARNING ENVIRONMENT

- FEEDBACK

- DEBRIEFING AND CLOSURE

- BUILD YOUR OWN TEACHING MODEL

> *"You cannot teach a person anything;*
> *you can only help him find it within himself."*
> — Galileo

Teaching can be magical. Good teachers or coaches create magic every day; it's almost as if there is no teacher and no learner, just the sport. All barriers to learning are conquered, all the power resides in the student, and learning becomes play. When this happens, electricity fills the air; the result is a learning experience packed with emotion, meaning, and value. This is what it's all about—building relationships that lead to learning and fun for students and teachers alike.

Models for teachers are abundant in texts and manuals. These ready-made plans are an attempt to provide a treasure map that, if followed, results in learning. They are built with the best of intentions, and many work well if the teacher connects with the model. Yet, like chasing a rainbow to reach a pot of gold, trying to follow a straight line on a multidimensional search can result in flat learning experiences ("smoke and mirrors") instead of results, and certainly no pot of gold.

The following three sections present the elements that, when artfully combined in their fullness, create the magical environment where connections are made and where learner and teacher are rewarded. The way to understand this special learning environment is through creating a personal model that takes both you and your learners into account. As you read in the previous chapter, learning is highly personal, and participation and practice are critical to creating connections in the brain. You will retain more of what you are about to read and experience if you get involved with the information,

manipulate it for yourself, and bring to it your own meaning.

As you read on, you will have the opportunity to create a personal model for yourself and then enrich it, adapt it, and share it with others.

Developing Trust

"Without trust there is no glue to hold relationships together."
— Schoel, Prouty, and Radcliffe
Islands of Healing: A Guide to
Adventure Based Counseling

Trust is the cornerstone of any productive learning experience. On one hand, students must trust that the teacher will "take care of them" and provide what is needed and wanted.

On the other hand, the teacher must trust that the students will make an honest effort to succeed and thus to help meet the goals of the teacher as well. Because both teacher and student risk failure in embarking on their shared experience, trust is key in working successfully toward the shared goal (fig. 3.1).

A lot has been written about the "introduction" of a lesson or learning experience. Most materials address the need to establish trust and a rapport with the student so that learning can occur. The idea often becomes too linear; establishing trust is not just something to check off the list at the beginning of the day before moving on to the next

FIGURE 3.1 Developing Trust

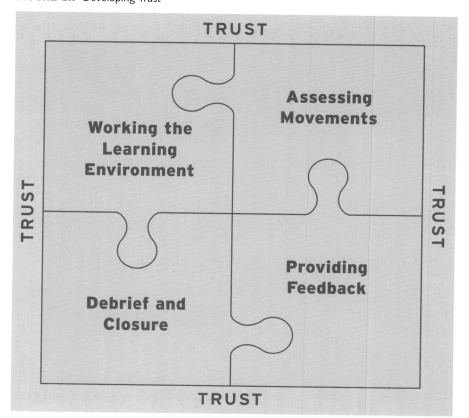

item. Real trust is built over the course of the entire experience and requires patience, thoughtfulness, and care.

When trust is nurtured, the result is an open, friendly, and confident atmosphere. Still, no matter the level of trust, a careless remark, poor decision, or ill-timed activity can blow it in an instant. As trust becomes deeper, the ability to push the boundaries becomes greater.

The nordic clinic was going great. Monica was feeling that she had accomplished something! She could tell that the skating rhythm was becoming smoother and more efficient, and she actually seemed to be going fast. It was awesome. The clinic was nearly finished, and the group asked Lars, their pro, to watch them one more time. As they powered past, Lars would call out words of encouragement, "Great! You're motion's really clean!" or, "Looking good; tremendous improvement!" But when Monica's turn came, his words for her were "Not bad, for you!" Monica came to a stop just off the trail, her head spinning. Did it mean that Lars didn't think she was as good as the others? Did it mean she looked really awful? Suddenly all the confidence that had been building was gone. Maybe it was hopeless. She was deflated.

CONFIDENCE

Research shows that your student's potential is directly related to your belief in...yourself! The most successful teachers and coaches have high expectations for both themselves and their students. They truly believe that they can get results based on their own knowledge, experience, and prior successes (table 3.1).

What does this have to do with trust? A lot! Who wants to take a lesson from someone who really doesn't believe that he or she can produce results? Have you ever taken a clinic or a lesson from someone who didn't make eye contact with you, spoke softly, and sounded wishy-washy? If so, it probably didn't inspire confidence.

TABLE 3.1 Keys to Confidence

- Experience
- People Skills
- Teaching Skills
- Technical Skills

So, what are the skills you need to feel confident? Are they technical skills, people skills, coaching skills, or a bit of all three? Spending time observing a master teacher at work can help build confidence in yourself. Gaining insight into your own learning style, and using that knowledge to get the training and information you need to feel confident, can bring increased success with your students and more fun at your job!

TEACHER EXPECTATIONS

"You are never given a wish without also being given the power to make it true. You may have to work for it, however."
— BACH

Confidence in your students' ability to learn is as important as confidence in your ability to teach. Studies of classroom teachers have demonstrated the amazing capacity for students to learn when their teacher believes they can. In one inner city study, a group of teachers were told that their students were gifted. The students were actually a group of challenged kids who had a history of behavior problems. At the end of the year, these troubled kids outperformed their peers in the control groups! Their teachers thought that they were gifted and treated them as such. They never gave up. (From

Rosenthal, *Pygmalion in the Classroom*). The old adage "You find what you are looking for" certainly bears out in this case.

The bus pulled into the resort's unloading zone, and Mordred was scheduled to welcome the 40 first-timers. As Mordred climbed onto the bus, she looked around at the expectant faces. She had given this speech a thousand times before: "Welcome to Mt. Snows-a-Lot! We're glad you made the choice to learn with us today. My name is Mordred, and I'll be organizing your group." As she looked around the bus, the dress, the style, the lack of fitness, and the "otherness" of those eyes struck her. These people were clearly not the mountain type. Mordred could tell just by looking, it was going to be a long day....

Have you ever had thoughts like this—looking at your students before you even ask their name and deciding they won't make it? The impact of this thinking can predetermine the failure of your students, a sort of self-fulfilling prophecy. Fortunately, this "first impression" cynicism is not inevitable and can easily be combated by viewing each new student or group as unique—just as you wouldn't want them to brand you with any negative impressions they have about snowsports instructors or teachers in general.

When people get to know each other on an individual basis, human connections are born and tolerance for people with a different perspectives, personality, and appearance is increased. As we learn about each other, we find out that what we have in common is usually far greater than how we differ. We all have hopes, dreams, fears, needs, families, jobs—we have the whole human experience in common.

Face the students, lean a bit toward them, and show attention by nodding and reflecting their emotions in your own facial expressions.

Remember to match nonverbal expressions with your words.

2. **Avoid Inappropriate Actions**

Don't do anything to indicate disinterest or condescension.

Don't discuss organizational issues or personal issues within earshot of your students.

Don't show frustration or disappointment.

3. **Remember Your Goals**

Relieve tension and take away any causes of stress or anxiety.

Determine the needs, goals, and motivations of the students.

Establish credibility for the experience and your ability.

"Welcome to Mt. Snows-a-Lot! I'm glad to meet you folks. I get nervous when I have to talk, so let's make some introductions all around and get you talking first! My name is Courtney James, and I'll be your pro today. I've been here for three years and have helped a lot of folks like you learn. Would each of you share your name, the real reason you're here today—even if it's just get out of going grocery shopping—and something different about you that will help us all remember your name. Why don't we start over here on this side of the group (shakes hands with the person on the end). Pleased to meet you! (looks into eyes). What's your name?"

Humor can help get you started, but judge your audience and keep the humor appropriate. Remember that nonverbal signals (body language, tone of voice, pacing, and volume) represent more than 90 percent of the impact we have on others.

In the realm of all that, every person you teach, no matter the age, gender, or nationality, has something in common with you. From the mundane to the sublime, it is there. Once you find out what it is, a basis for a true relationship is born.

By embracing a sense of anticipation about who your students are, why they are standing in front of you, and what you can learn about your sport from them, the barriers slowly recede.

BREAKING THE ICE

"Actions speak louder than words."
— SILBERMAN (PEOPLESMART)

The idea of "breaking the ice" has true meaning in a world where new faces can appear and disappear from the teacher's radar screen every few hours. Building relationships with 30 new people daily is exhausting, but can be exhilarating as well. If you have the interpersonal tools to get off on the right foot, the positive results will build your confidence and expertise (photo 3.1).

So, what are those skills? Learn to listen actively, use questions to gain a deeper level of information, and observe and interpret body language. Did you ever take a clinic or lesson from someone who didn't greet you, seemed disinterested, or stared at you? Probably not one of your best learning experiences. Following are some basic actions to help you connect more easily.

1. **Make a Positive First Impression**

Be well groomed.

Make comfortable eye contact and express genuine interest

Use students' names when addressing them.

Smile (sincerely).

Shake hands (if appropriate)—firmly but not overbearingly.

Assess the emotional state of the student: excited, apprehensive, etc.

Ask questions that give the student a chance to speak, and to give you a chance to listen and watch for important cues.

Listing

Listening

"You can see a lot, just by listening."
— Yogi Berra

Listening well requires clearing your mind from distractions. When you take care to do this, it shows respect for your students. It means that you put everything else out of your mind and really pay attention to what your students are saying, and how they are saying it (fig. 3.2).

When you actively listen to a student, you are listening with the intent to find something in the learner's past experience that you can use to aid learning. To begin, repeat in your own words what you have heard the student say. This is an opportunity to find out if you misunderstood. It also lets the learner know that you're paying attention, which invites further and deeper discussion.

Responses that show a lack of empathy for the emotion or issue being expressed can shut the door on further or deeper involvement of the learner. Reflecting the appropriate level of feeling in your response is also a key. Either overestimating or underestimating the level of the student's concern can be almost as harmful as misinterpreting the underlying emotion (anger, sadness, joy, fear, excitement, fatigue).

Questioning

When establishing rapport with students, it is important to ask questions about why they are there, what they hope to accomplish, and any prior experiences they have had. These questions are not meant to obtain rote answers, but to provide you with much more. When phrased carefully, the questions can help you

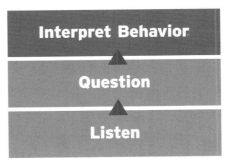

FIGURE 3.2 Active Listening

Interpret Behavior

▲

Question

▲

Listen

assess a student's feelings and attitudes about learning, the resort, and themselves. Three basic types of questions can help get at the information you need:

- **Closed Questions**
  Limit discussion and are used to elicit information or confirm understanding and agreement: "What's your name?" "Is this your own equipment?" "How many days have you been on the snow so far this year?"

- **Open Questions**
  Used to initiate a discussion or gain information about a customer's insights and opinions: "Which drills were the most helpful to you today?" "How does that turn shape feel compared to the ones we tried earlier?" "What movements are you still uncomfortable doing?"

- **Generative Questions**
  Provide insights to your students' level of commitment, the value they place on learning the snowsport, and their emotional response to the lesson, your teaching style, and their progress: "Why did you decide to take up this sport?" "What could we do in the lesson today that would really get you excited?" "How do you think it will feel when you're able to handle steep slopes, deep powder, and bumps?"

PHOTO 3.1 Express genuine interest in your students.

Using questions to create opportunities for active participation by students can help get them involved and invested in the process. As they share bits of information about themselves and their thoughts, they create neural connections that link an emotion and value to the experience. The greater the involvement, the higher the value. Questions can also be used to help calm anxious students and get their attention focused on you and the lesson.

INTERPRETING BEHAVIOR

Interpreting behavior is a complex skill. Although some of your students will share similarities with you and your values and beliefs, many more will not. Understanding those who are different from you is a challenge every pro must face. Different needs, styles, and backgrounds can make it difficult to determine what motivates these learners, but finding the answer is critical.

Silberman (2000) lists three essential skills that can help teachers interpret behaviors of their students: (1) evaluate their goals, (2) assess their personal styles, and (3) be cognizant of their differences. This can be difficult in a short time frame, but with practice you will learn to recognize the cues to help unlock the reasons for their behaviors.

Goals

According to Silberman, we all pursue three basic goals: control, connection, and competence. Some people have a high need to be in control due to their makeup or background. Some readily yield control to others.

Connection is the need to be involved with others, to feel supported and appreciated. Most people want to be included, but some seem intrusive while others choose to stay withdrawn. Still others seek connection in disruptive, or unacceptable ways. These may be the people who have low

self-esteem and feel they won't get connection from positive behaviors. Rather than get none, they choose the negative behavior to get attention.

People who are most concerned about competence want to show mastery to themselves and others. In the extreme, students with this focus may be hesitant to try something new for fear they will fail.

To interpret these goals effectively, you must remember your own goals, which form the lens through which you view others. If you have a strong need for control, you may not allow your students room for expression, producing negative behaviors. If you have a high need for connection, you may seem overbearing to your students and cause them to withdraw. If you have a need to show competence, you may overwhelm your students with your demonstrations and cause them to stop trying.

Personal Style

People are different. What a boring world it would be if we were all the same! Yet these differences, unless appreciated as just that and not as flaws, can be misinterpreted and either slow or prevent a relationship from building. As you get to know your students, recognizing their personal styles will help you interpret their behaviors.

In 1920, Carl Jung postulated a series of preferences for human reactions. which he called "function types" (described in Kiersey and Bates 1984, Please Understand Me). In the 1950s, these ideas resurfaced as the Meyers-Briggs Type Indicator. This is an inventory that measures individual functions in 16 parameters, based on the original work of Jung. This test is now widely used internationally. The preferences are organized into four scales, each with two preferences (see table 3.2).

The result of the test is a four-letter code that describes the

personal style of that individual. If you're interested, refer to Kiersey and Bates (1984) for a description of the 16 groups of people represented by the four-letter combinations.

You probably will not be able to cope with trying to address all 16 types in each clinic or lesson. The purpose of presenting this information is to make you aware that you will encounter many types of individuals in terms of focus, learning, decision-making, and reaction to externalities. If you are having difficulty reaching some of your students, they may simply be responding according to their personal styles, which may be in conflict with your own style.

Silberman (2000) describes how to interact more effectively with the eight basic personality categories:

- **Extroverted (E)**
  Let them think out loud.
  Try to respond to them quickly.
- **Introverted (I)**
  Give them time to think. Don't overwhelm them with questions.
- **Sensing (S)**
  Show them evidence (details, examples). Be practical, realistic, orderly.
- **Intuitive (N)**
  Give them the global concept first and let them ask for details. Tell them the challenges or benefits of an idea.
- **Thinking (T)**
  Be calm, concise, logical. List pros and cons of alternatives.
- **Feeling (F)**
  Be friendly and get to know them before getting down to business. Show them how an idea will be of value to them and others.
- **Judging (J)**
  Set a timetable and stick to it. Give advance warning of changes.
- **Perceiving (P)**
  Be flexible, allowing for options and changes. Bring in new information and ideas.

TABLE 3.2 Jung's Functioning Types			
Where do you focus your attention?	**How do you learn?**	**How do you decide?**	**How do you orient to the outer world?**
Extroverted (E) energized by the outer world	**Sensing (S)** by attending to facts, data, the "givens"	**Thinking (T)** through logic and objective standards	**Judging (J)** by being structured, organized, decisive
Introverted (I) tuned into your inner world	**Intuitive (N)** by attending to possibilities, overall patterns, the "big picture"	**Feeling (F)** through values and inner harmony	**Perceiving (P)** by being flexible, spontaneous, adaptive

Don't let this information overwhelm you. Just remember that the different types exist, and try to reach out to students in several different ways instead of only presenting the information in the way that worked best for you. Through time, you will develop a sort of sixth sense about the various types, how to recognize them, and how best to connect with them.

Recognition of Differences

A seemingly infinite number of factors influence the make-up of the individuals you relate to every day. These may include innate factors such as birth order, intelligence, stature, physical prowess, physical appearance, and gender. Cultural and religious background can overlay other influences such as social interactions, world-view, sense of time, sense of self, and basic values. Economic status will often determine attitude and expectations. Finally, age differences can affect both the physical and social aspects of learning. Differences in the eras in which students were raised can have as much effect on their attitudes and behaviors as differences in their bodies have on performance.

Again, the purpose of presenting this information is not to bury you with under an avalanche of facts to be memorized, but rather to create awareness that the variability among students is almost limitless. Quite literally, no two people are alike—

not even identical twins! Keep this in mind when trying to understand the motivations, wants, and needs of your students and when trying to build an effective connection for learning.

GETTING THE LEARNER INVOLVED

New teachers are often worried about what they are going to do in the clinic, rather than what their students will do. As a result, important clues that could help the teacher succeed are lost. In the first few moments of a lesson, students often reveal their true motivation for embarking on the learning experience, allude to fears or apprehensions, and share insights that can help the teacher determine how they will learn best. This may include everything from hobbies to family life and previous lessons. All this can be missed if the teacher is not vigilant in actively listening and staying attentive to this important information.

In fact, listening to your students describe precisely what they are looking for, how they learn best, and what experiences they have had in the past will begin to develop an atmosphere in which they work with you to develop a course of action. Getting the learners to talk about their experiences will help form a trusting partnership. As you question your students and listen actively to their responses, they become part of

determining the direction of the clinic. Suddenly, you are no longer there to provide the action plan; you are there to provide direction as they get involved in their own plan of exploration and discovery.

PREVIEWING

Probably one of the best ways to establish trust is to let your students know what is coming. Some learners really need to know how long the lesson will be, where they are going to go on the mountain, and whether they will have any breaks. This information helps them focus on learning instead of wondering where they will end up, if they will be able to make a restroom stop, and if they need money for lunch.

Students who know and understand the basic format of the clinic are more likely to contribute—even if the contribution consists only of anticipating and moving more efficiently from one part of the clinic to the next. Previewing is the act of describing, in a general way at the beginning of the lesson, what the students can expect to do and accomplish. As the clinic progresses, it is important to revise plans with the group and keep them informed about the schedule, tactics, and changes. This is critical for decreasing tension and reaffirming trust.

SUMMARY – DEVELOPING TRUST

Trust is established over the course of the entire learning experience. It must be nurtured from the moment the student is greeted until you say goodbye. While trust is built slowly, it can be destroyed in an instant with a careless word or action. To build trust, teachers need to be trustworthy; they need to have confidence in their ability to meet the needs and goals of their students. They must also hold their students in high esteem, show them respect, and anticipate their success.

Asking the right kind of questions, listening actively to the answers, and learning to interpret behaviors will contribute to your ability to build trusting relationships. These practices will involve the learners in the process and increase the value they place on the experience.

Assessing Movements

"Movement analysis is nothing more than describing movements and understanding their relevance."
— AASI Snowboard Manual

To help students improve at their chosen sport, you must first compare their current level of proficiency with their desired level. This can be accomplished with three basic questions:

1. Where do we want to go?
2. Where are we now?
3. How do we get there?

The artful coach is able to weave these three components together seamlessly and help students feel good about their accomplishments. It is of utmost importance that your expectations and judgments about what is "good" be replaced with a quest for what the student thinks is "good." A student might want to ski with feet together, or ride with arms touching

TABLE 3.3 Understanding Your Student's Goals	
Where are you now?	Where do you want to go?
"I'm sort of intermediate. I can get down anything, but not stylishly."	"I want to look better skiing/riding with my friends."
"I can carve on blue slopes pretty well. I'm fast."	"I want to get into the half-pipe or be able to handle bumps."
"I get frightened when I have to go fast or try a steeper slope."	"I want to be able to have fun with the family instead of holding them back or scaring myself."
"I'd say I'm advanced—steeps and bumps are no problem."	"I'm going on a helicopter trip to the Bugaboos and I don't want to embarrass myself."

the snow. In these cases, the real goal may be to look stylish or "cool." Most likely, the coach will proceed differently in helping meet these goals than with different goals. Only when you understand what your student is really trying to accomplish will you be able to enhance performance and increase the fun factor.

A final note of caution: A clinic in snowsports is fluid by nature. Circumstances change as learning proceeds. Goals you agree upon at the beginning of the clinic are very likely to change, depending on conditions and the student's progress. As you develop deeper relationships and begin to understand the connection between the mind and movements, be open to changing contexts and ready to make adjustments.

WHERE DO WE WANT TO GO?

The first step is to understand how accomplished a student feels at the outset of the lesson. This may have nothing to do with your own standards; your student's perception may be higher or lower than what you will assess. However, the context of the student's ideas will help you provide the appropriate tools and motivations for traveling the path to improvement (table 3.3).

The next step is to get moving. Your students want to move, so use it to begin to assess where they are. Here are some guidelines to help you get the ball rolling.

- Warm up on a less-than-challenging trail—and a familiar one, if possible. Be careful to avoid snap judgments. If you notice something in particular, whether positive or negative, remember that it's only the first run.
- Provide a simple, clear task so your students feel comfortable.
- Let them know you will be watching, but keep it low key: "Before we move on, it is important that I watch how you move at this point. Then, we'll decide how to proceed together."
- Watch your group or student from as many vantage points as possible: below them, behind them, and beside them (while they go by).
- Ask follow-up questions to assess the context of the movements you saw: "Was that a typical run for you?" "Did you feel the sensations you described to me earlier?" "Do you need some more turns to get going, or was that comfortable for you?"

PHOTO 3.2 Take a first impression "snapshot" of your learner.

BRIAN W. ROBB

WHERE ARE WE NOW? (WHAT DO YOU SEE?)

As you observe the students, try to get an overall picture of what's happening. Basic information may include comfort level, equipment set-up, snow conditions, and turn shape. Once you have this overall impression (photo 3.2), use your own personal plan to observe movements (table 3.4). The following ingredients are critical to developing your plan:

1. Know and understand the movements that really matter in your sport. (Refer to your sport-specific manual.)

2. Use your own learning style preference to help you process what you see. Are you more comfortable observing from whole to parts, or from parts to whole?

TABLE 3.4 Assessment Checklist
What do I choose? There is so much.
☐ **Arms low**
☐ **Feet close**
☐ **Balanced**
☐ **Skis edged**
☐ **Effect of equipment, etc.**

3. Evaluate what you see in the context of its influence on the student's performance. Assess what changes would have the desired result. This is the art of discerning cause-and-effect relationships in movement patterns.

Whatever method you use, be sure to eventually focus on specific movements that are relevant to your student's stated or implied goals.

A Sample Plan for Observation

To begin, take a holistic, first impression "snapshot" of your learners. What strikes you? For example, are they at ease or tense? Working hard or taking it easy? Athletic or sedentary? Is clothing or equipment enhancing or impeding performance? First impressions are powerful, but keep an open mind. Before you decide on the technical approach or solution, determine whether a simpler fix is indicated: a flatter trail, a clean pair of goggles, or boots that fit.

The most basic way to begin narrowing what you observe is to categorize and prioritize your observations into:

■ balance and stance
■ turn entry
■ turn shape (fig. 3.3)

Peter Howard, Eastern Examiner, National Certification Committee

Focusing on these three categories will help you discern the root of just about any performance challenge for your student and lead you to more specific observations and analysis.

Snow Tool Performance

As you continue to observe, focus on the chosen snow tool. Is the student getting a smooth ride or a rough ride? Is the snow tool of choice dictating the scene, or is the student? Once you have this overall impression, it's time to get specific with the performance

FIGURE 3.3 Edging is evident in turn shape.

of the snow tool itself. Refer to the respective technical manuals for complete descriptions of the possible and desired "snow tool performance."

Edging Movements

Your observation of the interaction of edge and snow can help reveal the application of movements (photo 3.3). An edge can carve an arc, create a smear, or not engage the snow at all. What is the effect on your student's overall performance?

Body Angles

As your student goes by you, get a side view. As you visually work your way up the body, you will begin to notice angles between body segments. Are the angles closed (small) or relatively open (large)? Are some closed and others open? Answers to these questions will uncover stance and balancing issues, how the skeleton is stacked (whether it is aligned with the forces at play), and how external pressures are being managed.

If you observe from the front or back, body angles and the level of the shoulders reveal which parts of the body are controlling edging and lateral balancing movements (photo 3.4).

PHOTO 3.3 Observe the interaction of edge and snow.

PHOTO 3.4 Body angles reveal which part of the body controls edging and balancing.

Turning Force

To find out how turning force is being applied, watch the torso and the legs (photo 3.5). Does the torso turn first, followed quickly by the legs? Does the torso turn first, and the legs only gradually realign themselves? Do the legs and torso turn at the same time but in opposite directions? Does the torso appear stationary while the legs turn? Take care not to be distracted by arm movements. Be sure to differentiate between movements that cause, or are caused by, other movements. Notice whether the head is carried smoothly and level.

Special Considerations for Children

When observing children's movements, you need to adjust your expectations in keeping with their degree of physical maturation (photo 3.6). Key issues are strength, length of limbs, location of CM, and development of fine motor control. Children's equipment can also hinder progress.

The key to understanding children's performance is simple: If the snow tool is gliding through the snow rather than pushing it or slipping sideways, the child is managing the equipment quite well (photo 3.7).

PHOTO 3.5 Turning forces are evident in torso and leg movements.

PHOTOS BY BRIAN W. ROBB

PHOTO 3.6 When observing children's movements, you need to adjust your expectations in keeping with their degree of physical maturation.

PHOTO 3.7 Is the snow tool gliding through the snow or being pushed?

PHOTOS BY BRIAN W. ROBB

Watch as many children as you can to gain experience in assessing this concept. You will soon learn when to focus your energy on coaching for change, and when to focus your energy on coaching tactics.

HOW DO WE GET THERE?

Now that you have assessed the current performance of your students and considered their goals, both expressed and implied, it is time to figure out a game plan. This is perhaps the most crucial time in your clinic. Your credibility with the student rests on your decisions here. Remember to keep the proper perspective and continue to work with the student, rather than evaluating and judging from a position of superiority.

Instructor #1: "Janey, don't worry about what you think you're feeling on the board. I'm the instructor, and you're paying me good money to teach you how to ride. Just do as I say and try to turn the way I've shown you."

Instructor #2: "Janey, was that run typical of the way you're riding now?"

"Yeah. I usually start getting out of control after a couple of turns. That's why I came today, so I can stay in control well enough to go in the trees."

"I have an idea that might help. It will mean focusing on the shape of your turns to help control speed. Are you ready to give it a try?"

The difference between these two instructors is obvious. In the first example, the teacher is all-knowing and not interested in the student's input. This puts all the responsibility for the success, or failure, of the lesson on the teacher and leaves the learner out of the equation. New teachers often think that they have to know it all and do it all; no wonder they are often overwhelmed!

In the second example, the teacher checks to see if the student is performing at the usual level and then works with the student to decide on the next step. If the student doesn't understand or a change needs to be made, the door is open for questions and clarifications. This attitude of shared responsibility makes the student an active participant and helps build the relationship.

Students may not be interested in all of the subtle movements that affect their performance; they just want to know how to improve. With experience, a coach can readily discern which movements have the biggest impact on performance and how successfully to share that information with the students.

Finally, assessing movements is an ongoing practice in any clinic or lesson. As a student tries new things, continue to watch and note progress, no matter how small. Point out the slightest improvement and help the student compare the associated sensations and movements with those at the beginning of the session. This creates a feeling of accomplishment, reinforces what was learned, shows how to recognize progress, and builds momentum for the next lesson!

SUMMARY – ASSESSING MOVEMENTS

- Where do we want to go? Be sure to take stock of student goals that are either expressed or implied. You may need to ask some careful questions to determine true expectations.
- Where are we now? (What do you see?) Be sure to make the effort to understand how accomplished your students believe themselves to be. This is then combined with what you observe to gauge actual skill level. Be open about what you see. Keep it in the context of what your student wants versus what you may value in performance.
- What's the best route for getting there? Involve your learners in determining the plan. Actively seeking their input will help them

buy into what you're doing and maintain an open, cooperative relationship in which they feel an equal part of the team.

Working the Learning Environment

"I love to learn, I hate to be taught."
— WINSTON CHURCHILL

Once you have assessed the current capabilities of your students and collaborated on goals for your session, it is time to start the learning activities. Of course, these activities will need description, modeling, indicators of how learning is progressing, and frequent reference to the original goals and expectations (fig. 3.4). Students who are active participants in this process will gain a deeper understanding of concepts, movements, and necessary changes. Unless the learner is actively involved in all levels of the process, true understanding may be sacrificed and relationships undermined.

Your challenge as a teacher, coach, or mentor will be to take the basic concepts described below and personalize them. Experience will help you determine when to apply the concepts, and at what intensity. After gaining an understanding of each part, you will need to step back and reassess the process as a whole.

FIGURE 3.4 Working the Learning Environment

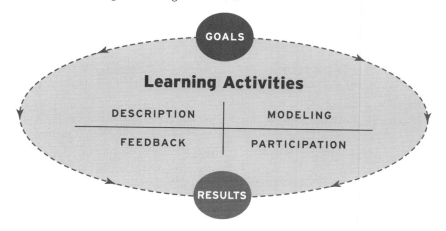

MASLOW'S MOUNTAIN

"Self-preservation is the first law of nature."
— Butler (ca. 1675)

As you continue to build the relationship with your students, you will find that they (and you) have certain basic needs. Abraham Maslow, a pioneer in the field of psychosocial and personality development, described these as a sort of pyramid, with the most critical needs (physiological needs) forming the base, and each successive need (safety and security, belonging, and self-esteem) representing higher layers. Each new layer can be added only when the previous, underlying need has been met. Maslow labeled the apex of the pyramid "self-actualization" (fig. 3.5).

Issues such as hunger, pain, cold, heat, fatigue, and other physical discomfort distract from any learning situation. Can you imagine learning to do flips on a trampoline if you had to answer nature's call, practicing the piano if you were shivering from the cold, or studying math if you were "bonking" from low blood sugar?

Be alert for body language that may indicate discomfort. Pay attention to things like time of day, temperature, and fatigue or low energy. Be aware of personal needs, such as bathroom breaks. Failing to monitor these needs can lead to some rather negative consequences! Creating an open and trustful relationship with the group can help by making the students feel comfortable to let you know about problems that are affecting them.

Josh had been working his eager group all morning. "We're nearing the base lodge. Wow! Can you guys smell those burgers? Who's hungry? I see that some of you are losing steam, but I want to practice a couple of those new moves on our way down. I have some water and trail mix in my pack. Let me know if you need something to tide you over. We'll be done in about 30 minutes, then we'll make a beeline for the lodge. Jamie! Was that your stomach I just heard? How about that trail mix! It'll help you focus and get the most out of the next few minutes."

Successful pros learn to minimize the potential for these types of problems. Before the lesson even begins, you might inquire whether everyone has been properly fed. Carrying a few snacks such as trail mix in your pocket or pack can avoid later disruptions of the lesson. You may need to break sooner than planned, but continuing the lesson with an individual or group that is running out of steam is not productive.

If the weather is unusually cold, windy, or potentially wet, check to see that everyone is properly attired: hat, gloves (mittens are better for children), adequate insulation, a wind shell, and/or a water-repellent layer. You also can manage the lesson to minimize discomfort during adverse weather, such as finding a more sheltered slope or take a longer break indoors to discuss concepts and practice movements on "dry land." If snow conditions on the preferred runs are too challenging, you can shift to easier terrain but substitute more challenging tasks.

The key is not only to be aware of discomfort among the students, but also to plan accordingly.

NEED FOR SAFETY AND SECURITY

As infants, the need for safety is surpassed only by the need for nourishment and shelter from the elements. This need continues throughout our lives, but as we grow and mature, we learn to avoid unsafe situations—except where a little danger can add to our enjoyment.

FIGURE 3.5 Maslow's Mountain

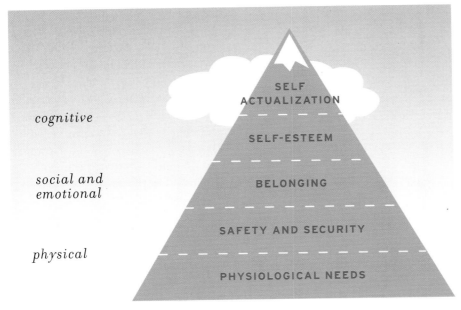

cognitive

social and
emotional

physical

SELF ACTUALIZATION

SELF-ESTEEM

BELONGING

SAFETY AND SECURITY

PHYSIOLOGICAL NEEDS

Truly unsafe situations, however, trigger fear responses that can swamp out other sensations and impede our ability to act or think. This applies to beginning snowsports students who are afraid of injury (fig. 3.6).

Taking Care of Your Students

One of your top priorities as a snowsports instructor is to ensure that your students are safe, and that they feel safe so they can focus on learning. Actions to take may include the following:

- Get to know your students' capabilities and limits so you can make good decisions about where to take them and what to ask of them.
- Have them warm up slowly.
- Be conservative in terrain choice, especially initially. Your group is only as capable as the weakest member.
- Be sure to take weather and snow conditions into account. Even the easiest terrain can be challenging under some conditions.
- Make a habit of checking the trail report and try to make your own warm-up runs on the slopes where you will be teaching.
- Take time of day into account. Fatigue increases as the day wears on, and snow conditions can

deteriorate. Plan accordingly.
- Resist the urge to cap off the day with the most challenging trail or task. While success can be exhilarating, a bad experience due to fatigue or poor conditions can be psychologically damaging.
- Monitoring where your group stops and stands. Consider other traffic when deciding where you take your students and what tasks you have them perform. Any activity that takes the class across a busy slope increases the potential for problems and can undermine trust.

Almost as important as taking these measures to protect your students is telling them about the measures. Students who know that you're watching out for their safety will be less worried and more able to focus on what you are saying or demonstrating. One of the main lessons you can teach your students is how to make decisions that will help take care of themselves in the mountain environment. This is something they can carry with them long after they've left your care. Remember—every lesson should include safety tips for your students.

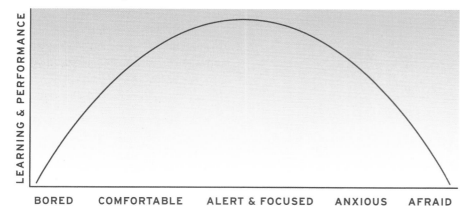

Dealing With Fear
"Between paralytic fear and lack of interest [we can provoke] motivation, interest, and awareness."
— ABRAHAM

It is critical to your success to recognize the difference between challenge and fear (photo 3.8). Fear is not only a serious impediment to learning, it also is one of the main reasons people choose to not continue in snowsports. To understand what your students may experience, try to remember a time when you were really afraid. Can you recall the physical state of your body? Do you remember your heart pounding and your senses heightened? Were you too scared to move or cry out? Was anyone there to help you through it?

Establishing a rapport with your students includes letting them know that it's okay if they feel and express anxiety about where they are or what they're doing. If they do, how should you respond? First, remember that no matter the cause and reasonableness of the fear, it is real and it is there. Acknowledge it. If you show that you understand and respect the predicament, the student is much more likely to listen and respond to you.

FIGURE 3.6 Learning and Performance

LEARNING & PERFORMANCE

BORED COMFORTABLE ALERT & FOCUSED ANXIOUS AFRAID

Next, determine how serious their reaction is. Since the physical reaction is a barrier to effective communication, establish a link through the senses.

"Karen, can you look at me?" (She can succeed at this simple task.)
"Can you feel that you aren't moving?"
"Yes."
"We're going to take this one step at a time. Okay?"
"Okay, but I can't move!"
"It's all right. We'll go across the slope. Just look in my eyes and listen to what I'm saying. I'm right here. I'll make the path, and you just glide toward me. You can stop as much and as often as you need, and I'll stop you when you get to me. Ready?"

In *In the Yikes! Zone*, Blakeslee (2002) provides a number of suggestions for dealing with your students' fears. One way of working with students who know that they are fearful in certain situations is to develop a list of "cue sounds" that link them to past successes. According to Blakeslee, "although an actual word can be used, its meaning is not as critical as its sound—its length, rhythm, forcefulness, and feeling. A spoken cue triggers the desired movements by translating the student's focus into a sound the body responds to, language that often elude the everyday logic of the intellect."

For best results, the sounds and responses can be developed before the frightening situation and practiced in a comfortable setting until the student feels ready to challenge the fear.

"Okay, what's the cue that has worked so well for you?"
"And soft."
"Remember to make it sound soft."
"Oh, yeah, and saaawwwffft."
"What does that make your body do?"
"It helps me let go of the old turn and start a new one."
"Can you say it with that same relaxed tone you had before? That's it. Now, when you say it, feel how your body is going to move. Can you feel it? Good, keep saying it. Here we go."

Another tactic for diffusing fear is to modify the task in a way that accommodates the student's fear. Often, it is helpful to introduce the task on terrain where the student is comfortable. The task should encourage the same movements and intensity the student will need for more challenging terrain (fig. 3.7). For students frightened of pitch, try setting up a situation where they are gently coerced into turning more across the hill, using turn shape to control speed. On gentle terrain, simulate the effect of pitch by having the student go straight downhill for as long as possible before beginning a series of rhythmically identical turns that gradually tighten and slow the student to a stop. In a comfortable environment, the student learns not only the movements needed but also the intensity required to face the steeps.

Learning to lower the task when attempting challenging terrain is even more important. When a teacher models specific, safe ways to appropriately lower the task, the student learns how to explore terrain on the edge of his or her ability without making movements that are less safe or defensive (fig. 3.8).

PHOTO 3.8 Steeps represent challenge or fear, depending on the person.

BRIAN W. ROBB

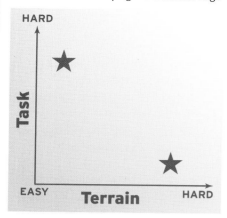

FIGURE 3.7 Developing the Individual Edge

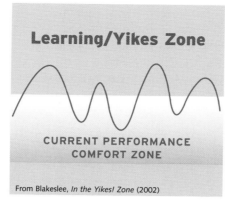

FIGURE 3.8 Understanding and Playing with the "Point of Failure"

Learning/Yikes Zone

CURRENT PERFORMANCE COMFORT ZONE

From Blakeslee, *In the Yikes! Zone* (2002)

NEED FOR BELONGING

Once your students have had their physiological needs met and become comfortable that they are not in danger, they need to feel that they belong. We all have an innate need for belonging, to be accepted and respected, whether as part of a one-on-one relationship or a large group.

With an individual student, show that you are equal members of the learning team. With a group, let them all know that they are equally important to you. Establish a personal connection with them as individuals, but also treat them like a team with common goals. Create situations in which they help or encourage each other and are invested in each other's success. Show them that you and the other students care about them (fig. 3.9).

NEED FOR SELF-ESTEEM

"People are at risk when they learn. This risk may be physical, social, emotional, intellectual, or spiritual in nature."
— JOHN CHEFFERS
SILVER BULLETS

Students who undertake a new sport, or any new task, risk a loss of self-esteem. In snowsports, this may be less obvious than risk of physical injury, but it can be just as important

a factor in learning. Loss of self-esteem can arise externally (being embarrassed in front of others or failing to meet expectations of a parent) or internally (reinforcing self-doubt or failing to meet one's own expectations). In their book *Inner Skiing*, Gallwey and Kriegel (1997) identified self-doubt, fear of being judged, and fear of being injured as the three major impediments to learning to ski; these also apply to snowboarding and many other sports (fig. 3.10).

For most people, the harshest critic they will ever face is their own internal voice. You know, the one that says...

- "Are you nuts? You're going to break your neck!"

- "Sure, you did it this time, but it was a fluke!"
- "So far the group seems to like you, but that's going to change when they see how awful you look trying to ski bumps."

As a teacher or coach, you need to be cognizant of each student's internal voice and whether it is hindering the process of learning. Keep students focused on the here and now, or on past successes and imagined future successes. Be positive. Avoid reference to past and imagined future failures. Set students up for small successes through skillful selection of tasks, terrain, and snow conditions, and describe any improvements you observe. By emphasizing positive changes, and giving them a positive emotional context, you help the student build a history of success that can be drawn from and added to.

Throughout this process, be careful to avoid statements that are judgmental; focus instead on objective observations:

- **Judgmental**
  "Those turns weren't very good!"
  Objective
  "Those turns didn't create the c-shape you were trying for. Remember to keep the radius of the turn consistent."

FIGURE 3.9 Need for Belonging

Comfort
Student is comfortable being vulnerable

+

Respect
Student and guide respect each other's skills and expertise

=

Trust
Student trusts guide and experience

From Blakeslee, *In the Yikes! Zone* (2002)

FIGURE 3.10 Self-esteem Risk

Sensations *usually uncomfortable* → **Awareness** *snow tool and body* → **Movements** *enhanced or replaced* → **New Sensations**

From Blakeslee, *In the Yikes! Zone* (2002)

- **Judgmental**
  "You aren't using your edge correctly."
- **Objective**
  "Your edge wasn't engaged at the start of the turn, so you slid through it instead of carving."

Objective observations deal with things that are external and controllable and give the student suggestions on how to improve. Judgmental statements deal with the quality of the effort and can trigger that negative inner voice.

When you recognize success and make sure that it is internalized and given emotional value, a history of success is built that can be called upon to guide the learner to higher levels of achievement.

EFFECTIVE COMMUNICATION

"Learning is experience. Everything else is just information."
— ALBERT EINSTEIN

To be a successful educator, you must be able to communicate skillfully with your students. They, in turn, must be motivated to listen so they can understand. While this point seems obvious, can you remember attending a clinic or an educational event in which you were bored, confused, or even angered because the speaker wasn't clear? Can you remember a clinic or lesson you took when...

- The pro just jumped right into a topic without explaining what it was about?
- The pro talked incessantly, and you couldn't get a word in edgewise?
- The terminology seemed foreign and difficult to grasp?
- You felt criticized? Or stupid?
- The pro never made eye contact with you, even when talking to you?

PHOTO 3.9 A demo is worth a thousand words.

BRIAN W. ROBB

- The pro said things such as, "Is that clear?" but gave no chance to answer?
- The clinic ended, and you weren't sure what the main point was?

These instances happen often in our daily lives. With a little effort, you can improve your ability to be understood. All it takes is a little empathy for what learner's experience and a little knowledge about how they view the world.

According to Silberman (2000), communicating well is a result of being able to get the message across, speaking directly, and including the learner in the message.

Get the Message Across

Getting necessary information to the students can be accomplished in many ways, and taking stock of your options is important. When you reflect on the specific piece of information you'd like to convey, also think about the best way for the learner to experience it. Combining a concise verbal description with some other sensory input is often helpful: "Let's review the timing for that turn. I'll come toward you, and you watch my pole."

In most cases, a demonstration is worth many words, especially for students who are primarily visual learners (photo 3.9). Equally important is that the students have a chance to get involved in activity as soon as possible. If you feel as though you are talking a lot, ask for permission to use a demonstration, or ask if they would like to show you and have you comment.

Another means of getting the point across is to use the terrain to illustrate for you. Setting your student up to turn on a knoll, or to feel the sensation when moving from pitch to flat or from one snow condition to another, are tools for exploring concepts and issues first hand.

Set your learners up to hear what you have to say and then summarize when you are finished. Try to remember an instance when you had to communicate something very important: "Are you ready for this one?" or "I need you to listen to me for a minute." When you have explained the concept or completed the lesson, bring closure by summarizing. The summary can come from you, or you can ask the students to summarize.

To liven up your speech, and add to the possibilities for mental connections in your learners, learn to paint vivid pictures with your words: "If your feet are lined up correctly during the turn, it feels like you're attached to a wall, just like a fly."

Speak Directly

Make your students feel comfortable, yet give them the real scoop. It can be tempting to cloud the truth or use evasive language in an attempt to avoid hurt feelings or questions that you might not be able to answer. Don't give in to this temptation.

Honesty is an important part of establishing a productive relationship with your students. This doesn't mean that you should speak the "brutal" truth—critiques should be put in a positive light. However, when students are discovering, they sometimes get lost on tangents. If they don't feel comfortable making observations or movements that are incorrect, they won't explore at all. You can keep the atmosphere ripe for exploration by looking at each wrong answer as an opportunity to try other ways of presenting the information. You may gain new insights for yourself and the group, or you might just help someone rejoin the main flow of the river after exploring a tributary.

Wyatt was trying to learn to control his speed. His typical way of slowing down was to twist his upper body as hard as he could to get his feet around quickly. In this way he could slow down, but not very comfortably or efficiently. He had trouble on blue squares, and wanted help. As Wyatt's coach was describing the concept of turn shape, Wyatt commented, "To make my turns that way, I just twist, and my feet end up pointed just like you said."

"That's interesting, Wyatt. Do you mean that you turn your feet? Or do you start your turn from your upper body?"

PHOTO 3.10 Talk *with* your students, not *at* them.

BRIAN W. ROBB

Asking this clarifying question gets Wyatt off the hook with his peers, who can see that he isn't doing as the coach described. It's also possible that the coach's description wasn't clear to others in the group besides Wyatt. In this case, it gives the coach a chance to clarify the description for everyone, while keeping Wyatt a positive part of the discovery.

"Good observation, Wyatt. Let's explore that concept. Try twisting your body through the turn, and then try using your feet first and see what happens."

In this way, the coach kept Wyatt involved and making learning connections, rather than interfering with the learning process by being judgmental or lowering self-esteem.

Finally, it is very important to make your body language consistent with your message. Make eye contact with each learner, and support the discoveries with encouraging expressions or gestures. These can include maintaining an open posture, nodding, standing nearby when new movements are tried, a thumbs-up, and an occasional touch on the shoulder, if appropriate.

Include the Learner in the Message

Good teachers talk with people, not at them (photo 3.10). Yet, including learners in the message does much more than just making sure they get to talk. It is important to speak their language and confirm their understanding.

Speaking the language of your students means using what you know about them to frame the experience from their perspective. Knowledge of learning styles, multiple intelligences, and sensory preferences are all tools you can use to engage your learners.

Using Learning Styles

Since it is almost impossible to figure out the learning styles and preferences of all your students, the key is to use as many tools as possible. With experience, you will learn to recognize traits and cues that help focus your presentation more closely. Still, as stated in previously, most people learn in multiple modes. A rich, varied presentation will help you engage all of the students (figs. 3.11 and 3.12). Bernice McCarthy has described the following four-step process:

1. The teacher, as initiator and motivator, conveys enthusiasm for the subject.
2. The teacher delivers the lesson content through description and demonstration.
3. The teacher steps back a bit to facilitate, nurture exploration, and ask provocative questions while the learner is tinkering, testing, and trying.
4. The teacher acts as cheerleader and facilitates independence, while the learner is adapting and creating anew.

Using Multiple Intelligence Theory

It is impossible to include all seven types of intelligence in every learning activity, but you can easily use more than one. When you know your own preferences, it is easier to go beyond them onto other, less traveled roads. For example, consider turn shape:

- **Verbal-Linguistic**
  "Your turn shape can vary, from a c-shape, to a j-shape, to an open s-shape."
- **Musical-Rhythmic**
  "For braking turns, think zhat, zhat, zhat; for longer turns, think zhaaaaa, zhaaaaa, zhaaaaa."

- **Logical-Mathematical**
  "Count the beat of your shorter turn. Then count a shorter or longer one to vary the shape."
- **Spatial**
  "Plan the shape of the turn you would like to make by spotting the trees on the side of the slope."
- **Bodily-Kinesthetic**
  "Pay attention to the timing of the turn you are about to make. What body part were you aware of? Can you lengthen that sensation? Can you shorten it?"
- **Interpersonal**
  "Pair up and watch your partner. Imitate their turn shape, and categorize it. Then reverse roles. Explore different shapes of turns together, and come back to the group and describe how you adjusted to make them different."
- **Intrapersonal**
  "Can you visualize yourself making short, snappy turns? Try that. Now, visualize the long, clean arc of a giant slalom racer. Try that."

Relax and have fun. The more varied your plan, the more exciting the results. Remember, these are only starting points that must be built and developed with each individual student in mind.

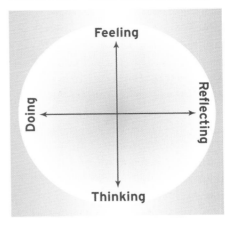

FIGURE 3.12 Flexible Modes of Learning

Using Sensory Preferences

Discovering a student's preferred mode of sensory processing will help you achieve effective motivation and communication.

- **Visual**—Many students learn best by seeing or watching. They store information in the brain as a picture and use imagery to understand new concepts. Someone who depends strongly on visual input may talk fast and will relate better to how something "looks" than to how it "feels."
- **Auditory**—Some students emphasize auditory cues in learning. They store information as a running commentary in their brains. Directions make sense if given step-by-step; other input (perceived as noise or interference) can easily distract. These students may ask and answer questions in their own brains as they learn.
- **Kinesthetic**—Other students have a heightened awareness of their bodies and how things "feel." They learn best by doing. This type of learner may need to experience the sensation associated with a type of movement or combination of movements to understand the concept ("This feels awesome!").

FIGURE 3.11 Flexible Modes of Teaching

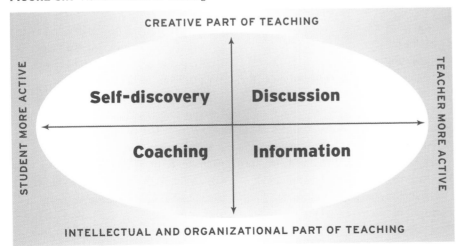

CREATIVE PRACTICE TIME

Although integral to the learning process, practice time is an under-utilized tool among teachers of snowsports. The initial excitement of correctly performing a movement leads the teacher and student to look to the next step up the ladder—a linear approach—rather than to practical application of the new skill. More than 300 repetitions of a new movement are typically required for true learning to occur.

To provide ample time for practice, first make your goals specific enough that you don't try to accomplish too much at once. Consider the example of adjusting the timing of weight transfer, or edge transfer, which has many variables for skiers and snowboarders alike. Aside from the mechanics of the concept are the considerations of conditions, terrain, and speed. No one would expect that once the first parallel turn is made on skis, or the first carve achieved on a snowboard, the learner will never regress to former tactics. Do you remember learning to drive a standard shift car? Just because you got it right in the driveway didn't mean you that you would get it right on a hill!

Practice time doesn't have to be just repetition and boredom. The variables themselves—conditions, terrain, and speed—can be adjusted endlessly. Seek the new sensations and practice describing them so they are assigned meaning and connection in the brain.

GROUP HANDLING SKILLS

Another variable at your disposal is the group environment. Rather than worrying about how to handle a group that is stationary, consider how to manage the group when they are moving and interacting. This can be the ripest learning time of all.

Pairs

Use pairs as a way of providing individual feedback within a group, but be careful that partners frame the feedback so that they are not attacking (or judging) each other or wasting time observations that are not useful.

"Christina, remember that you are only allowed to tell Shayla if you saw her head move up and down. The same applies to Shayla when it's her turn to observe."

"Christina, as the observer, your job is to determine exactly where Shayla first engaged her edge during the turn."

Using pairs requires a few special considerations:

- When pairing students, consider carefully how to group them. It can be beneficial to pair someone who is struggling with someone stronger. Or, it can be good for stronger performers to be together to elevate each other's performance. Rotating random pairings is sometimes good for group dynamics and helps them get to know each other. At other times, pairing by similar equipment, size, or speed capabilities may be important. Consider the task and pair accordingly.
- Always give a framework for feedback so the focus stays positive and productive. The observers' understanding can be improved by watching their partner. Make sure they are aware of this.
- Frame the boundaries of the experience, the beginning and ending zone. Also, watch for their safety. Learners can often become so engrossed in a task that they lose focus on external surroundings.
- Move from pair to pair and check performance. This is a great opportunity to work with someone who is struggling, or someone who is more advanced. (In a group setting, focusing on one or a few individuals can cause the others to feel neglected).
- If you have an odd number of students, you can pair up with one for a bit to give special help, and then ask them to join another duo while you circulate.
- Allow enough time and terrain for both partners to experience both roles.

Subgroups

Groups of three or four can be useful in discovering answers to more open-ended challenges.

"Explore as many different speeds as you can, and then we'll get back together and see which speed was best for this movement."

"Stop three times before the end of the slope. In each section, use a different turn shape. When we regroup we'll see which we liked and which were more challenging."

There really are no right or wrong answers, just experience to be gained and a chance to internalize the sensations through discussion. Again, it is important to frame the physical boundaries and to move from group to group to be sure they stay on track.

Whole Group

When you want to observe the whole group, one tactic is a line rotation. Begin by asking the group to space themselves along the trail's edge. Then, the person at the top of the line performs a given task to the end of the line. The others all take their turn when they become the top of the line. Repeat while moving the whole group down the slope. This is best done on an open slope to provide room for other customers. The teacher can function in a number of ways in this activity.

- Set a task for all to emulate; this is a good way to provide a good visual image.
- Maintain control by changing the task each rotation.
- Move from student to student as the line continues to give feedback.
- Set aside an uninterrupted time for movement analysis.
- Provide more or less control as desired. You can specify not only the task, but the speed and radius. However, the terrain will change. You can let the group decide the appropriate speed and tactics given their piece of terrain. You can appoint different leaders to change the task. These possibilities are infinite.
- Get the whole group involved by asking them to watch a specific movement or individual. Their observations can either be discussed at the end of the exercise, or the group can call out specific instructions to the students going by.

  In either of these cases, be alert for issues of self-esteem, as discussed previously.

Private Lessons

If you are coaching a private lesson, you still have some creative options for keeping the student practicing and involved. Try alternating the "you try and I'll stand and watch" tactic with descending side-by-side or switching leader and follower. When the student is the follower, have her or him stay a fixed distance behind. These tactics will help your students bring the mechanical focus of learning a new movement into the wholeness of application.

TEACHING ACTIVITIES

Teaching activities encompass everything from the initial steps for learning a new movement, to specific drills for refining already learned movements, to holistic activities that challenge and solidify performance.

Everything we do to initiate and explore movement belongs in the realm of teaching activities. Some movements, or combinations of movements and sensations, lend themselves to a step-by-step progression. Others require holistic activities such as varying speed or intensity. Activities may proceed from general to specific, from details to the big picture, from concrete to abstract. The past experiences of the students add yet another dimension to the mix and can help anchor their learning. Teaching activities are your tools for bridging the gap between where the student is now, and where she or he wants to be at the end of the lesson (fig. 3.13).

In *Technical Skills for Alpine Skiing*, Ellen Post Foster (1995) makes some practical suggestions relative to drills, progressions, or games.
- Use drills and games to achieve technical goals.
- Explain why a drill is being used and how it will be beneficial.
- Relate drills and progressions to actual situations.
- Relate parts-oriented experiences to holistic applications.
- Make sure the drills are appropriate for the ability and maturity of the students.
- Include adventure, challenge, and excitement in each experience.
- Provide ample practice time. This is essential for improvement.
- Encourage precision and accuracy in executing drills to maximize their effectiveness.
- Use the Skill/Drill/Hill Formula: **skill** = what you want the student to learn; **drill** = the situation you create to encourage learning; **hill** = the appropriate terrain for success.

Using the list above, think about some of the teaching activities you have used or have participated in. Write down variables on those themes by adding a different element from the chart. For example, if you teach people to turn using a step-by-step approach, is there a more holistic approach you could try? If you have people turn using visual cues, are there other sensory cues that might work better for some learners? If you typically challenge your groups by taking them to more difficult terrain, how you might also challenge them on easier terrain?

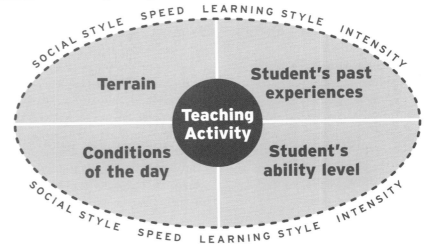

FIGURE 3.13 Selecting Teaching Activities

The teaching activity is the learning potion taken from the cauldron of variables among students and conditions. The possibilities are infinite, the variations exciting, and the challenges never-ending. This is where master teachers practice their craft.

LEVELS OF UNDERSTANDING

The goal of teaching is learning. Yet, how can you tell if someone has learned something? Can you remember a situation in which you thought you learned something but were unable to repeat it when the clinic was over? Did you ever study something for a test or exam and realize after the test was over you could no longer remember the information? It is important for students to receive value for their time, effort, and money—in other words, to have learned. To truly have learned, whatever they take away must have personal meaning attached so it will last (fig. 3.14).

Years ago, Benjamin Bloom (1956) listed a series of developmental stages through which a learner progresses. These move from superficial and rather narrow toward a deeper, integrated meaning. As you engage your students in learning activities, continually evaluate their progress with respect to these stages. Questions to ask yourself along the way are:

- What will they say when asked "So, what did you do in your lesson?"
- Will your students be able to apply the skills they learned after they leave you?
- If they have difficulties again, when you aren't there to coach them, will they be able to break it down and work on the parts?
- Have you given them ample time to discover what acquisition of the new skill will accomplish for them over a range of variables such as speed, terrain, and conditions?
- Have you anchored the learning with value? Will they say the lesson was worth the time and the money they spent?

Consider Troy, the advanced skier who finally decided to take a clinic. He was discouraged because he felt out of control on the steeps. At the close of the lesson, he was just as discouraged. His group had focused on turn shape the whole day but had stayed on what he felt were very easy trails. Although Troy enjoyed himself and felt comfortable in the lesson, he was unable to connect what he had learned to what he needed.

Willa, Troy's best friend, had joined a different group. She was ecstatic! She was just getting good enough on her snowboard to enjoy intermediate terrain but was uncomfortable on advanced slopes. Yet, she was bored and wanted some way to get better without scaring herself on the steeps. Her instructor coached the group on some freestyle skills and then showed them why they were useful in all-mountain riding. They spent time practicing and had a blast! In fact, they even went on an easier black diamond trail, and Willa felt in total control! She gave her instructor a big tip and signed up for the next class.

Feedback

Feedback can make or break a learning experience. It can provide direction to guide the learner on a course, it can reinforce positive change and redirect unproductive movements or actions. Feedback can also influence the student's feeling of worth, belonging, and comfort. On the physical side, feedback is like the map the student follows to reach a destination.

Emotionally, feedback keeps the learner in the game. By reinforcing efforts and framing experiences, the teacher keeps students involved and vested in the value of the process itself. For feedback to be effective, it must be both welcome and informative.

MAKE SURE YOUR FEEDBACK IS WELCOME

To make sure your feedback is welcome, an atmosphere of trust must exist between teacher and student. The teacher must show respect and empathy for the learner's experience, moment to moment. Inappropriate feedback can destroy any trust that has been building. Feedback is more likely to be welcome if the teacher asks for permission, makes well-timed observations rather than judgments, and checks to be sure the feedback was understood.

During a task or activity, a good teacher is vigilant in observing performance and guiding the student toward success. However, unless the student asks for input, you should ask permission before giving advice or offering feedback.

"Arnica, I think I see something that's contributing to your difficulty with this task. Shall I share it with you?"

FIGURE 3.14 Learning Activities

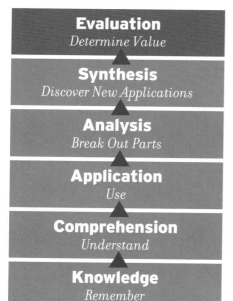

After obtaining permission for feedback, determine the optimal timing for each student. Most will prefer it directly following performance, especially if it is positive so that behaviors are reinforced. Feedback can also be effective during performance or after the entire group has completed the task.

Timing is everything. Given too soon, feedback can be distracting and interrupt performance. Too late, and sensations are forgotten, making changes difficult to implement. Again, when in doubt, ask the learner to help you determine the best timing in each instance.

"Forrest, I just noticed something! Do you want to hear it now, or would you rather keep trying to work it out for yourself and talk about it later?"

To be sure that the feedback is not judgmental, focus on observed behaviors or changes and how they relate to performance. This keeps the comments objective and separated from the self-worth of the student.

- **Judgmental**
  "Marie, you didn't change a thing. You're still letting your skis slide through the turn."
  Objective
  "Marie, your right ski is flat when you start the turn. Can you feel that?"

- **Judgmental**
  "Warren, your heelside turn is really ugly."
  Objective
  "Warren, your back ankle is locked on your heelside turn. Think about flexing it in the transition."

- **Judgmental**
  "Nicholas, you still aren't getting the correct turn shape."
  Objective
  "Nicholas, the turn shape was tighter than the last time. Can you make it still tighter?"

Feedback must be understood to be effective. Check frequently with your students ensure that they are following your guidance and staying on track. After offering feedback, ask for a response. Was it clear? Was it helpful? Do they know what to change? Is more information needed?

"Does that make sense, Stefan? Would you like to try it?"
"Well, I'm not really sure how to engage my toe edge earlier. How do I do that?"

Listen for cues that your feedback has been misunderstood. This gives you an opportunity to rectify the situation before trust is broken.

"Cody, I didn't mean that you didn't try, I meant that I'd like you to try again. I know you're giving it your best, and you're getting closer. To really nail it, though, you need to repeat the movements as many times as possible. Okay?"

MAKE SURE THE FEEDBACK IS MEANINGFUL

To be meaningful, feedback has to be heard with an open mind. Your students will be more open to your suggestions and retain more of what they hear if you begin with something that is positive. The positive framework helps keep the student motivated, but only if it is useful information that will help to gain the goal. To have the most impact, make your feedback specific and brief, and offer positive steps for improvement.

Debriefing and Closure

"Teachers nurturing an understanding of underlying concepts are more effective and less stifled in their approach. Utilizing mental aspects of learning and performing, this new generation of instructors is able to promote greater enjoyment and more lasting successes for their students. Leading the [student] beyond the mechanical realm... is the real challenge of modern [snowsports] schools."
— ABRAHAM

"Don't be dismayed at good-byes. A farewell is necessary before you can meet again. And meeting again, after moments or lifetimes, is certain for those who are friends."
— BACH

The close of the session is critical to the success of the experience. Here is the lasting impression, the connection to value, the motivation to continue practicing and learning and improving. Perhaps you can remember a lesson when you were just getting involved, and you heard, "Oh! Time's up. I have another appointment. Bye!" What a missed opportunity.

The goal of any good summary is to include "What?" "So What?" and "Now What?" in the wrap-up. This enables you to pull all the learning together into some nuggets for the students to take with them. This format also provides a final chance to involve and engage your students. Remember the old adage about public speaking: "Tell what you're going to say, say it, then tell what you said."

Begin by gathering the group around you and asking them what they learned. Make it fresh and open-ended. Leave room for them to remember their excitement and their challenge:

- "What was your favorite activity?"
- "What was the turning point for you in the lesson?"
- "What held the most value for you today?"
- "What are you taking away from this experience?"
- "What would you repeat if you had the opportunity?"

These are open-ended questions with no right or wrong answer. They provide the students a chance to reflect and connect to their own meaning, rather than have you recite what you think they accomplished. Of course, you can ask further questions in your debrief to gain more information for both you and the student. This is the "So What?" where deeper meaning and insight are gained. Usually these center on emotions or sensations:

- "What did you like about that activity?"
- "How did you feel when you accomplished that?"
- "Why did you choose that run as your best?"
- "If that was too challenging, how would you make it more inviting?"
- "So, if you did this again, what would you do differently?"

These questions and their responses lead into the "Now What?" closure. It is important to leave your group with internal direction. This is the part that ties the package with a neat little bow. "As a result of this experience I can, or I will...." These are powerful words that give your student a sense of worth and meaning:

- "What will you do now, as a result of this experience?"
- "What can you do now that you couldn't do before?"

Do you remember a lesson or clinic experience when you didn't feel you were making progress? Were you motivated to keep trying? Chances are that if you were, your coach encouraged you with feedback that gave you a positive result, no matter how small. This was real feedback, and realistic. Not "You got it" when you didn't, but "I think I saw the inside edge roll a bit sooner; try it again." If you kept going, it was because you had reason to hope that you would eventually accomplish the task. If you gave up, it was because you decided you weren't going to accomplish your goal. That power is in the coach's hands and heart. If the coach gives up, the student doesn't have a chance. Remember that the next time you feel like your student isn't performing.

Build Your Own Teaching Model

"Although people do not [always] behave congruently with their espoused theories [what they say], they do behave congruently with their theories-in-use [their mental models]"
— CHRIS ARGYLIS, HARVARD UNIVERSITY QUOTED IN SENGE, THE FIFTH DISCIPLINE: THE ART AND PRACTICE OF THE LEARNING ORGANIZATION

Now that you have read and experienced the ingredients that make up good coaching, it's time for you to manipulate and play with the information you've absorbed. This will facilitate the formation of new connections in your brain that link the information with your thoughts and beliefs. When the new connections are made, you may find yourself changed, reassured, or challenged and excited to try new ideas and practice new behaviors. Your mental model determines not only how you make sense of the world, but how you take action in response.

EVOLUTION OF A PRACTICE

- Questions instigate language.
- Language instigates models.
- Models instigate thinking.
- Thinking instigates understanding.
- Understanding produces competent performance.
- Competent performance produces lasting self-esteem.
- Self-esteem produces motivation for new learning.

From National Academy Speech, Ed Joyce, (April 2000)

Now, if you are bursting with ideas about what your model should look like, skip the material in this section and start designing! Also, refer to the PSIA (www.psia.org) or AASI (www.aasi.org) websites to see some models for creating a learning environment. Take time to share your model with others and modify it as your ideas about teaching expand.

Stuck for where to start or what to create? First, try some of the brain-stretching exercises presented below. Next, read through the suggested steps to guide you through the process.

BRAIN STRETCHERS

The important thing about brain stretchers is that they help change your perspective, or make new associations, or create metaphors that alter your emotional response toward something. The activities below will help frame a new perspective on your view of teaching.

Simile Search

The object of this game is to think of as many things unrelated to teaching snowsports as you can, and then associate them with teaching. Here's an example:

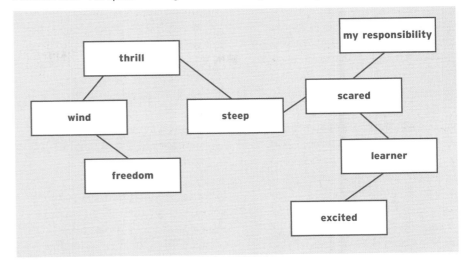

FIGURE 3.15 The spider-webbing exercise encourages new insights.

Teaching winter sports is like driving a race car because the more gas you give it, the faster it goes. But, if you give it too much gas all at once, you'll flood the engine. If you give your students too much "gas" or information all at once, you'll flood their "engine" (their brain) too. If you take a corner driving too fast, you'll flip the car. If you get going on an idea in a clinic and then suddenly change the focus, you may flip your students.

Are you ready to try some similes on your own? Here goes!

- Teaching skiing is like fishing because...
- Teaching snowboarding is like swimming because...
- Teaching someone to ride a snow-bike is like climbing a tree because...
- Teaching someone to use outriggers is like planting a garden because...
- Teaching a survival course on nordic gear is like a day at the beach because...

Sticky Connections

The next brain stretcher is called "spider-webbing." This is a way to free your brain to associate with as little conscious thought as possible. It is fun to do in a group because the group synergy will often produce funny yet unexpected results (fig. 3.15).

Begin by taking a word and placing it in the middle of the paper. From the word draw a line connecting it to the first thought that comes into your brain. If that thought stimulates another one, connect that one and so on. If it stimulates two thoughts, connect them both. This way you can follow your brain's "free association" on paper. As you travel down this path, you may discover hidden thoughts, ideas, values, meanings, and images that you hadn't looked at quite that way before.

Here are some words to get you started. Try...

- Teacher
- Coach
- Learning
- Experience
- Relationship

Metaphor Mania

When you create a metaphor, you take a subject or idea and use it in place of another to suggest a likeness between the two. Metaphors often elicit emotion, which anchors an expression as an image or sensation. Examples could include:

- The ski roared through the snow (ski compared to a lion).
- The wind danced on my face (wind compared to a dancer).
- The view embraced me (a scenic view given human quality and emotion).
- Her words chilled me (words given weather qualities).
- My fear ran away (emotion given physical qualities).

Try making your own by describing a run you had. As you go back through the paragraph, edit it to include the metaphors. You can vary them or try for a theme. Remember, the key is not to judge what you produce, just to do it and see where the thought process leads. You don't have to become the next Ernest Hemingway!

STEPS FOR BUILDING YOUR OWN MODEL

The best way to begin your model-building experiment is to think about it as constructing a model airplane or car. First, gather all the needed materials. The materials would consist of the major points of the previous chapters. What are those?

- **Developing Trust**
  What were the high points; what held meaning for you?
- **Assessing Movements**
  Can you make any global observations about the materials presented?
- **Building a Learning Environment**
  What conditions need to be present for students to make gains in their learning?

- **Using Learning Activities**
  Can you come up with a simile or metaphor that works for you here?
- **Providing Feedback**
  What is your key attitude toward feedback?
- **Debriefing and Closure**
  Can you think of questions or statements that will help students remember the lesson and look forward to the next one?

Next, give some life to the components you have identified above by associating them with some emotion or value. Then, begin organizing them in priority or manipulating them as objects. Try writing each key component on a piece of paper and arranging them in order on a table. What does the shape look like? Does it remind you of anything?

Ta Da! Now, share your model with others and see the variety of possibilities. It will also help you see what is important to other teachers and coaches. If you are still stumped, you can refer to the examples in the online appendix and see if one of those stimulates you. You may also submit your model by sending it to the national office. Send a hard copy to:

PSIA-AASI Education Department
133 South Van Gordon Street
Suite 101
Lakewood, Colorado 80228

Some submissions will be periodically posted on the websites. Another tactic is to try building your model with a friend or group. See how many different possibilities you can dream up.

When all models are created and the ink is dry on the page, what really matters is what has been stimulated in you. Has the process of building your model helped you understand learning and teaching in a new way? Have you been stimulated to think about how you teach and learn? Are you motivated to explore new resources and gain deeper insights?

MENTAL MODEL CREDO

1. The effectiveness of a teacher is related to the continual improvement of the teacher's mental models.
2. Don't impose your favorite mental model on your students. Mental models should lead to self-concluding decisions to work their best. Self-concluding decisions result in deeper conviction and more effective implementation.
3. Better mental models enable adjustment to changed conditions or circumstances.
4. Multiple mental models bring multiple perspectives.
5. Groups add dynamics and knowledge beyond what one person can do alone.
6. A teacher's worth is measured by her or his contribution to the mental models of others.

Adapted from Senge (1990)

"Observing the successes of others can show us new possibilities, expand our thinking, trigger our creativity. But their experience can never provide models that will work the same for us. It is good to be inquisitive; it is hopeless to believe that they have discovered our answers."
— Wheatley and Kellner-Rogers
A Simpler Way

Working Relationships

chapter 4

- WE'RE ALL IN THIS TOGETHER
- JOINING THE TEAM
- RESOLVING CONFLICTS WITH CUSTOMERS AND TEAM MEMBERS

We're All In This Together

The number one goal of any resort is to provide a fun-filled experience for its guests. All staff, from maintenance workers to senior managers, make their decisions based on this vision. Although coaching students on the hill may seem to be a separate activity from resort operations, a lot of teamwork is needed to set the stage for the clinic experience.

From lifts to snow, from tickets to equipment, from lunch to hotel rooms, the extended members of your team help to meet the needs of your students. Like your extended family, these teammates often do their jobs in a place remote from where you are. You may hardly give a second thought to their roles unless something is amiss. Yet, their contribution is fundamental to your job. Imagine teaching a snowsport without snow. Imagine teaching without lodges, lifts, or rental gear. You notice if the snow quality isn't right, the rental gear doesn't fit, or the lift smacks you in the back of the knees. You are in ecstasy if the grooming is perfect, the burgers are juicy, and the administrative staff gets your schedule booked correctly.

On the other hand, those who perform the other tasks at the resort notice your effect on the resort as well. For many, snowsports instruction is their introduction to the mountain lifestyle. New visitors to the mountains rely on your expertise to make a lasting impression; the resorts rely on you to keep the visitors coming back—

PHOTOS BY BRIAN W. ROBB

COURTESY OF WINTER PARK, COLORADO

FIGURE 4.1 Numerous variables contribute to the guest's overall mountain experience.

MOUNTAIN OPERATIONS
Lifts
Snowmaking
Grooming
Maintenance

MOUNTAIN SERVICES
Safety Services
Guest Services
Tickets
Human Resources

The Mountain Experience

MARKETING
Sales
Merchandising
Public Relations

ACCOUNTING
Control
Information
Services

and bringing their friends. You provide the image and soul of the mountain lifestyle. Even those who don't participate in lessons see pros on the mountain and gauge their performance against what they see. Staff members in other departments support what you share with the guests: the mountain experience (fig. 4.1). You can enhance your personal success by building relationships with other staff members at the resort.

Josie was a new snowboard pro. She loved coaching and, most of all, loved snowboarding. She took advantage of every training opportunity, connected with her students on a personal level, kept a meticulous teaching log, and set goals of reaching her Level II. Her students had begun requesting her for private lessons, and she was getting great tips.

One morning, she took her private student out for the first run. The grooming was not quite what she was used to. She and her student came across a ridge of snow that had been pushed up along the edge of the trail. Since the light was flat, it was a little tricky. "Wow! This stinks! I can't believe they let those groomers get away with that!" When the lesson was finished, she fumed about the conditions to the other instructors in the locker room.

The next morning, she was called to her supervisor's office. Apparently, her student had fallen later in the day and had indicated that the grooming was at fault—and that Josie would support this.

Josie let her team down. By not being aware of the whole resort, she endangered not only herself, but also her fellow staff members.

Jeremy was a successful pro at the same mountain. He had a private lesson scheduled the same morning as Josie. However, when Jeremy and his client came upon the ridge left by the groomers, he remarked, "Hey! This is an opportunity to challenge your skills. Let's see what we can learn here."

Following the lesson, Jeremy went to his supervisor to report what they had encountered. The supervisor called the grooming department and asked if they could help in any way.

By avoiding blame and accepting the responsibility for communicating possible danger, Jeremy may have helped prevent unnecessary accidents and gained rapport with the groomers. Now, if Jeremy has recommendations for slope maintenance that will help his students, the grooming staff will be more likely to listen and act.

What's in all this for Jeremy? If the resort is in trouble, his job and direct line to the mountain experience could be in trouble. When he accepted the responsibility for communicating with his teammates, he increased the service level of the resort and his value as a staff member.

Perhaps even more important than your extended resort family is your immediate resort family. This is the team of pros who share the locker room, give you assignments, train with you, and accompany you on mountain explorations. Although it may seem that you don't actually teach with them, how you interact can determine your success or failure over the long term.

One day, Duggan was bringing his group to the base for lunch. His route took him through the beginner area, where several learner groups were eking out shaky turns. As his group carved their way through the others, another pro called out to him. He looked back to see her struggling with a crying child and the other kids in various states of uprightness.

Duggan figured that she would never know if he had in fact heard her plea for help. So, he continued on his way to the base area to bring his group in for lunch. "I've done my share on the learning slope," he thought, "and anyway, she must be nuts to have so many kids up there."

Later that week, Duggan was assigned a group of raw beginners. Just before lunch, one of the students suddenly fell in the middle of a turn. Duggan rushed over to discover that the student was cut and bleeding. It wasn't bad, but Duggan needed to get Heather down the mountain right away and didn't feel that the others could keep up. Just then, Duggan noticed another pro heading in for lunch with her group of kids. He yelled for help, and the other pro stopped.

"What's up?"

"Well, Heather has a bit of a cut and needs to get to first aid. Could you shepherd my group to the bottom along with your kids? They can wait for me at the bell while you head back up. Would that be okay?"

"You bet! See you later."

As Duggan headed in with Heather, he considered what had just happened. He recalled his own actions a few days prior and resolved not to refuse to help someone again.

Joining the Team
"Together Everyone Achieves More"

Team players join a group with an open attitude toward the possibilities of others. They recognize that the reason a team is powerful is the diversity of its members. All members of a team bring their life experience to bear on any given activity or issue. Good team players are able to successfully blend their talents with those of their teammates. They are open to the resources that other members provide and contribute to an atmosphere of dialogue rather than advocating one side or the other. "They act as if they are part of the group's pool of knowledge, skills, and ideas and are successful in getting others to act that way themselves (Silberman 2000)."

BE AWARE
As in the story of Duggan, it is important to be aware of the needs of others on your team. By noticing that cleanup chores need to be done, or that someone needs a hand, or that someone needs advice about which clinic to attend, you send a message of cooperation and respect. This message goes through you to other members of the team and ultimately reaches the guests at the resort (fig. 4.2).

FIGURE 4.2 Resort employees must work as a team to ensure that every student has a positive, memorable experience.

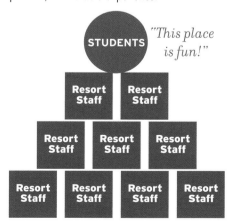

MAKE CONTRIBUTIONS
Awareness is just the first step. Once you are aware of a need, step in to help. Imagine a soccer team that consisted of nine players who tried to shoot goals. That would result in lack of defense and a lot of goals by the other team. It's the same on the slope. If you happen to be available when someone else gets caught up in a task, make the contribution and help the team.

Here are a few contributions you can make toward the team's success:
- Assist others when you're able and it's appropriate.
- Share information.
- Be objective when discussing different viewpoints.
- Bring conflict into the open rather than acting as a go-between.
- Show appreciation for the efforts of others.
- Share the credit for success with your team.
- Use humor to relieve tension.
- Be aware of the effects of your actions on others.
- Ask for help when needed, and give help when asked.
- Be alert to the talent of others and use it for the team's advantage.

ACKNOWLEDGE THE CONTRIBUTIONS OF OTHERS
Finally, to really contribute to a team atmosphere, remember to give recognition for the efforts and contributions of others. A simple "thanks" is usually all it takes to cultivate positive feelings and enthusiasm. To see if you are part of a great team, ask yourself these questions:

Resolving Conflicts with Customers and Team Members

"There is no such thing as a problem without a gift for you in its hands. You seek problems, because you need their gifts."
— BACH

Conflict and chaos can be positive to growth and learning. Upheaval and loss of control can give us new perspectives and make us appreciate new things. Although conflict itself is often painful and difficult to face, the result can be a fresh start.

We are in conflict when our own concerns and needs are incompatible with those of others. Coaching snow-sports offers some interesting possibilities for conflict. Some specific challenges you may face are:

- Resolving scheduling conflicts.
- Challenges with specific assignments.
- Confronting gossiping or back-stabbing colleagues.
- Dealing with challenges regarding job performance.
- Coping with dissatisfied supervisors or students.

STYLES OF CONFLICT RESOLUTION

In any conflict, behaviors can be described along two basic gradients. The first is your assertiveness level, or the extent to which you attempt to satisfy your own needs (fig. 4.3). The second is your level of cooperation, or how hard you try to satisfy the other person's needs (fig. 4.4). According to Kenneth Thomas and Ralph Killeen, creators of the Thomas-Kilmann Conflict Mode Instrument (a questionnaire that assesses conflict management savvy),

Are you...
- Achieving something?
- Moving forward?
- Learning?

Do you feel that you...
- Belong to something greater than just yourself?
- Are accepted and respected?
- Fit in?

Are you...
- Contributing?
- Appreciated for what you bring to the group?
- Needed?

If you can answer positively to these questions, you're undoubtedly a solid member of a strong team. If you are in doubt about any of the questions, review the chapter to determine if there are adjustments you can make for yourself or suggest to your teammates.

We all have a basic need to achieve, belong, and contribute. These are what give meaning to our work. When we attain them, we send a message to our clients that reflects fun, excitement, and a positive attitude.

FIGURE 4.3 Meeting Needs

these two basic tendencies in personal behavior can be used to define five specific methods for dealing with conflict.

1. Competition is the act of being assertive to the point of caring only about having it your way. While healthy when used to spur performance, competition can be very damaging in situations that require teamwork:

Bart: "I see on the schedule that you've assigned me a bunch of beginners and given the advanced students to Lance. I'm technically much better than Lance, so I should be given the advanced classes."

While Bart may indeed be technically better than Lance, this aggressive approach creates hard feelings within the staff, and the supervisor won't appreciate having to change the schedule just to feed Bart's ego.

2. Accommodation is the opposite of competing. It consists of putting the needs of the organization or another person above your own:

Blair: "I like teaching advanced students, and I see that I'm on the schedule for that, but I'm willing to trade with Bart if that will make everyone happy."

The supervisor will be grateful to Blair for helping resolve the conflict and putting the good of the school ahead of personal desires. Blair will undoubtedly be rewarded on future schedules.

3. Avoidance is deciding to not get involved in a conflict in order to "choose the battle" or wait for a better time and place:

Serene: "I see I've got beginners all day. That's fine" (while thinking, "I hate teaching beginners, but I don't want to create friction. I'll talk to the supervisor about it later").

The supervisor will appreciate not having to deal with the issue right then and will gladly assign Serene some advanced students on the next schedule.

4. Collaboration consists of actively working with the other party(ies) to find a workable solution:

Tasha: "The schedules always seem to create a lot of angst about beginner classes. Maybe you should have a staff meeting to remind everyone that teaching beginners is critical to the success of the resort and that it's part of what you expect from us as professionals. We could also try to come up with a long-term rotation so it isn't an issue every morning."

The supervisor will appreciate Tasha's desire to work together and with the staff to avoid problems in the future and will view Tasha as someone with good ideas that go beyond just being a good instructor.

5. Compromise means that both parties are willing to give up something to achieve a mutually satisfactory result:

Tyree: "I'd be willing to teach beginners all weekend if I could get more advanced classes the rest of the week."

FIGURE 4.4 Methods of Managing Conflicts

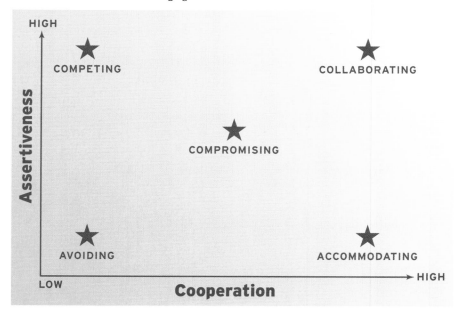

The supervisor will almost certainly agree to this "win-win" situation and give Tyree special consideration when other issues arise.

No matter what type of conflict resolution you usually use, the reality is that no one method is well suited to every situation or person you will encounter. The key it to preserve a healthy working relationship with your peers and supervisor while not creating situations that are so negative for yourself that they adversely affect the attitude and energy you bring to the students.

BE POSITIVE

It often is difficult to remain respectful and considerate when in conflict with someone. The tendency is to see the other person as the problem rather than to look objectively at the issue. People who are able to separate the behavior of the other party from the source of the conflict are more successful at controlling negative emotions and keeping a proper perspective.

IDENTIFY THE SOURCE OF CONFLICT

Describing a conflict will help bring the issue to light so the opposing parties can take a step back and view it openly. In this process, it is important to know what kind of conflict is causing the challenge. In *Managing Work Place Conflict*, Jean Lebedun (1998) identified four basic causes and categories of conflict:

- **Facts or Data**
  Incorrect information, or misunderstanding.
- **Process or Methods**
  Same goals, different ways of getting there.
- **Purpose**
  Different goals.
- **Values**
  Different basic belief systems (often the most difficult).

Defining the true essence of the conflict helps to remove extraneous issues that may cloud the issue and narrow the choice of responses (fig. 4.5).

STAY FOCUSED ON THE REAL ISSUES

Conflict resolution can get derailed for a variety of reasons. Sometimes, we get caught up in irrelevant details or relate the current conflict to past issues. Emotion can cause us to refuse to listen to the other person or understand what they really want. Sometimes we just haven't figured out what we want ourselves.

Often, the key to resolving conflict is to understand the reasons behind the positions being taken. These usually are based on personal interests or the reason we took the position in the first place. When common ground is discovered, respect is restored or reinforced and a solution is easier to see.

Sonja was a kids program manager who felt strongly about the quality of her program and wanted the families who attended to get the best possible experience. Sonja's manager would often make jokes at staff meetings about the kids program. "Hey! If you don't show up to the banquet on time, I'll assign you to the kids program for a week."

After mulling over the issue, Sonja asked her manager if she could talk to him in his office. "Josh, I hate the jokes you make about teaching kids. It seems like you don't value kids teachers or the kids program. I think it sets a bad example, demoralizes anyone associated with the kids program, and makes it hard for me to get volunteers from the adult school when we're overrun. I'm really angry about it, and I think we should make some changes around here to make the kids program more on an even par."

"Whoa, I didn't mean anything by those comments, but you know as well as I do that threatening any good pro with teaching young kids will put the fear of you-know-what in them! It's all in fun and will get them to be more responsible."

Sonja was outraged at these remarks but realized that Josh had probably never taught kids himself and looked at the kids program as glorified baby sitting to be assigned to the newest and greenest staff members. She also believed that Josh really wanted quality for the whole school, not just his own programs. "Josh, what is your biggest dream for your program? What are your goals?"

"Well, I want my staff to be responsible and provide the guests with a quality experience. That would lead to recognition from management that we were doing our share to get people involved in the mountain lifestyle and keeping them as resort customers."

"Josh, did it ever occur to you that we have the same goals, and that the kids program is a big part of your own goals and dreams? Families represent about 60 percent of our business, and most of your clients have kids in our programs. Do you think they'll participate in your sessions if they aren't satisfied that their kids are safe, happy, and learning something?"

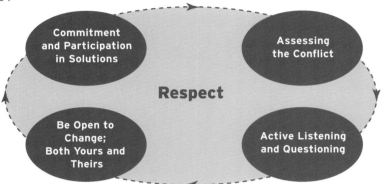

Sonja's questions dug for a common interest with Josh. Through her questions, she tried to show him that they wanted the same things, thus encouraging a change in his behavior. Reaching a point of common interest requires mutual respect and a belief that the other party will listen and respond.

In conflict, we can use the same tools we use when we coach effectively. Actively listen to the other person so their needs are really clear (not just what you think they are). Ask good questions that will help the other person see your ideas and their own more clearly. Be open to change. It is important to be aware of subtle body language that can show you they are ready for change, or that you are. Involve the other person in the solution, so the conflict is truly resolved rather than put off.

SUMMARY – RESOLVING CONFLICT

Conflicts are resolved in one of five ways: competition, accommodation, avoidance, collaboration, or compromise. Each approach is appropriate in different situations. We all have a tendency to use one or more styles based on our assertiveness and spirit of cooperation. The key to resolving conflicts is in appreciating other points of view and listening for common interests upon which to base solutions. From there, the end result relies on individuals to participate in solutions.

Part 2
Responsibilities

To be a success, you must be aware of safety issues, live up to students' expectations, provide value, and understand your responsibilities. Mountain sports are inherently risky. People who choose to explore the alpine environment must accept this fact. However, when they do so under the care and guidance of a resort professional, the risks are minimized. They are not eliminated under any circumstances.

Beyond safety are other expectations that provide value for the time and money spent under your tutelage. Snowsports teachers, by the very nature of their relationship with their students, can make or break the resort experience. This is our "hidden contract" with the resort and those who go there to learn.

- CREATING LASTING MEMORIES
- THE MOUNTAIN ENVIRONMENT
- PROFESSIONAL DEVELOPMENT

Creating Lasting Memories

chapter 5

- WHY PEOPLE DON'T COME BACK

- YOU MAKE THE DIFFERENCE

"Argue for your limitations, and sure enough they're yours."
— Bach

Your resort is in the business of selling service. While the mountain itself is the attraction, the amenities and facilities are important to the experience, shaped by interactions with staff members. From the moment a hopeful resort enthusiast picks up a phone or logs onto the web to make a reservation, until the gear is packed and the trip home has begun, hundreds of interactions with employees have contributed to the overall impression of the resort. Each staff member can help meet a guest's needs.

As a snowsports teacher or coach, many things are beyond your control: weather, facilities, snow conditions. However, things you can control such as your ability to work with other staff members and your supervisors, your ability to interact in a positive way with each guest you encounter, and your own personal contribution to resort operations can make all the difference.

By the time you greet guests for a clinic, they will have already had to pass through a variety of hoops. Consider a family that arrives at a resort for the first time. Imagine bringing two small children through multiple parking lots, with gear, only to find they must walk another quarter mile to the children's center. Or consider the group of friends who decide to learn to ride a snowboard, only to find that finding their way around and renting equipment causes them to be late for the lesson.

PHOTO 5.1 Focus on how the resort looks through the guest's eyes.

BRIAN W. ROBB

Take a moment to walk through your resort and see it from your customer's eyes (photo 5.1). Familiarity with the common challenges your students face will give you added patience and empathy in the meeting area and allow you to help them solve any problems that could threaten their experience.

When your guests know you understand and appreciate what they go through, they will be more able to move on to the learning experience. When you show them how much you love not just your sport, but your resort, they will realize that their effort was worth it and will want to be part of that experience again and again.

Nathan was excited to finally get to go to the famous Mt. Snows-a-Lot. After making his reservation, he knew it would be special. Even the reservation agent remarked before he hung up the phone, "You're going to have a great vacation! You'll love it here. We all do!"

When he arrived at lodging check-in, a hotel employee noticed his broken suitcase handle and offered to fix it during his stay. Nathan was pleased. His binding had also broken on the plane. The check-in agent called the shop, and they had a pair of skis just like his. They let him use them at no charge and called the airline to figure out what to do about his broken binding. Nathan was amazed.

Two things that could already have disrupted his vacation had been taken care of. Wow! By the time Nathan arrived at his clinic, he was smiling and relaxed. He was focused and ready to enjoy the mountain.

Lorie was excited to finally take the kids to Mt. Far-Away for a real family break. She called ahead to try and arrange everything for her two children prior to their arrival, but they told her not to worry, just show up early.

When Lorie checked in, she was given a long list of things to get and places to go with her boys. By the time they were signed up and in the programs, it was noon, and Lorie's first day on snow was half gone. The staff was smiling and tried to be helpful, but they didn't know what each other was doing and often gave her the wrong information. Most of all, they didn't seem to really care about her.

Lorie was exhausted. By the time she got herself into a lesson it was past 2 o'clock. She growled at the instructor and quit after a run or two. Her pro never had a chance.

Why People Don't Come Back

According to surveys, more than two-thirds of customers who decide not to return to a place of business do so because they feel an attitude of indifference from the staff (MacNeill, Customer Service Excellence). The following list summarizes more survey results about why people don't come back. Have you ever been on the giving or receiving end of any of these behaviors (table 5.1)?

Someone who leaves your resort angry will tell an average of 9 others, and 13 percent will tell another 20. At that rate, your resort's potential losses increase exponentially. So, how do you affect the service at your resort for your own benefit? What can you do? Consider these ABCs of service for snowsports pros (table 5.2):

- Try to see your resort, your work area, and your appearance through the customers' eyes. Make sure your image is one your customers will want to emulate or have their children aspire toward.
- Show genuine interest in who the customers are and why they are there. Help them clarify their goals and map out a plan for attaining them.
- Actively listen to their responses and let their input shape the experience. Give them a sense of involvement and control.
- Foster a feeling of accomplishment and a desire for future challenge and learning. Help them want to come back.

TABLE 5.1 These behaviors are sure to discourage guests from returning.

PROBLEM	BASIS
Perceived apathy; atmosphere that staff doesn't care	No eye contact when guests come to meeting areas or sales areas
	Staff appearance (uniforms) not professional
	No empathy with guest issues
A feeling of unimportance; staff members don't treat each customer as an individual with specific needs	Teaching on auto-pilot to group; no individual feedback
	Forgetting names
	Rude and/or condescending behavior
	Negative reactions when guests are late
	Negative reactions when guests end up in the wrong level for ability
The "runaround"	Sending guests rather than taking them or going for them
	Not calling ahead for the guests to be sure they will be taken care of
Everything is complicated or slow; nothing is easy	Questions and concerns met with answers such as: "Oh, I don't think that's possible." "We don't do that here." "Not at this resort." Rather than: "Let me see if we can handle that request." "We've never tried that before!" "What would it take to do that?"

- Point out the progress they made and help them understand the next step toward their longer-term goals.
- Create a sense of belonging and a comfortable place to return to.
- Recommend restaurants, movies, and other activities that will round out their experience.
- Show them the short cuts; give them a sense of being "insiders."
- Show them that you appreciate them as people as well as clients. Respect their choices and opinions.
- Take suggestions and input thoughtfully and graciously. Let them help you to improve.
- Acknowledge when a mistake has been made and begin steps to correct the situation.
- If they are planning to return, let them know when you will be available. You are a friendly face, a known entity, and a consultant.

TABLE 5.2 The ABCs of service. These feelings create lasting memories.

☆ **Achievement**
☆ **Belonging**
☆ **Contribution**

You Make the Difference

When students leave your lesson, what will they tell their friends? Try to imagine what you want them to say and coach toward that goal. Generate stories to get people talking about your coaching and your resort. This is what creates a reputation for good service and gives your students lasting memories of valuable experiences.

"Check it out," Sean said to his friend Kristan at the end of the day. "When my goggles cracked, my instructor called the mid-mountain shop to be sure they had the kind I needed and asked them to hold them until I got there. He then changed the lesson to stop by the shop on our next run, and I got them at a big discount. How cool!"

A resort environment contains all kinds of potential roadblocks to the perfect day for a customer. Though many of these are out of your control, you are the last line of defense—you can make or break their day. Moral of the story: Give them something to write home about!

The Mountain Environment

chapter 6

- MANAGING RISK IN THE MOUNTAIN ENVIRONMENT
- SHARING THE MOUNTAIN ENVIRONMENT

> *"In nature there are neither rewards nor punishments. There are consequences."*
>
> — R.G. Ingersoll

Managing Risk in the Mountain Environment

When you venture onto a snow-clad mountain with snow tools attached to your feet, certain risks are unavoidable. Creating an atmosphere of risk awareness and providing basic information on safety are among your responsibilities as an instructor (fig. 6.1).

Coaching risk awareness is pragmatic. Different groups require different tactics. Young children need specific boundaries and close supervision. Their lack of experience and youthful exuberance can make them less aware of risk, and their developmental stage affects sensory awareness, mental processing, and the physical ability to react. With young children, the instructor should monitor risk for the group and redirect inappropriate behavior.

Older children and adults can be provided basic information and examples of appropriate actions and their results, then allowed to reach their own conclusions about risk and safety. This does not imply abandonment, just freedom to explore, knowing that the leader will gently redirect or point out risk when it arises.

PHOTOS BY BRIAN W. ROBB

FIGURE 6.1 When students feel safe and are having fun, the learning quotient is higher than ever.

Safety + Fun = Learning

Practical advice and experiential learning are appropriate for all ages. A group of 6-year-olds can act out the parts of Your Responsibility Code while on a warm-up break indoors. They can also watch the actions of others on the mountain and see the results. An example of this is looking uphill before starting down the slope. They can experience this in a real sense, and verbalize the consequences of forgetting. Drawing the attention of your group to an event such as a near collision and asking questions about the consequences can solidify the meaning of risk.

YOUR RESPONSIBILITY CODE

Safety is always a serious concern on ski mountains. The National Ski Areas Association's "Head Up" safety campaign promotes responsible mountain behavior. By following the seven simple rules—the "do's" of safe skiing—and sharing them with your students at frequent intervals, you'll be doing a big favor to yourself and everyone else on the slopes. These rules, also known as Your Responsibility Code, are endorsed by NSAA, PSIA, AASI, and NSP (table 6.1).

CHOICE OF TERRAIN

Choosing the right terrain for learning is another of your responsibilities as an instructor. This decision affects both the physical and emotional safety of your group. Making the right choice depends on your understanding of the ability level and emotional state of your students and of slope conditions.

Ability Level

You can only go as far as the weakest member of your group. If you are questioning the choice, err on the side of caution. You can always keep more advanced students challenged with a more difficult task, but you can't make a bump run less bumpy!

Kevin's group wanted to go to The Jaws of Death. They were all 8 years old, pretty capable skiers, and game to try new things. Yet one boy, Luke, was always at the back of the group. He was good enough at slow speeds, but when

TABLE 6.1 Safety First

Your Responsibility Code

1. Always stay in control.
2. People ahead of you have the right of way.
3. Stop in a safe place for you and others.
4. Whenever starting downhill or merging, look uphill and yield.
5. Use devices to help prevent runaway equipment.
6. Observe signs and warning, and keep off closed trails.
7. Know how to use the lifts safely.

Other guidelines to make for fun, hazard-free skiing:

Body Basics

- Slather on at least 15 SPF broad-spectrum sunscreen, regardless of whether the day's sunny or cloudy.
- Drink frequently to avoid the dehydrating effects of high altitude.
- Layer with breathable, water-wicking layers than can be added or subtracted with changes in weather.

Serious Signage

- ● **Green Circle:** Easiest trails and more mellow slopes.
- ■ **Blue Square:** More difficult trails and intermediate slopes.
- ◆ **Black Diamond:** Most difficult trails and vertical slopes.
- ◆◆ **Double Black Diamond:** Expert skiers only.
- △ **Caution Triangle:** Heads up, this terrain may contain hazards.
- ⊘ **Red Octagon with slash through skier:** Trail or area is closed. No skiing allowed.

Learn Your Limits

- Don't take that last run when your legs have turned to Jell-O.™
- Ski at your own level. Test your skills to improve, but know when you're crossing over into dangerous territory. Ski patrollers say this is the number one safety issue at resorts.
- Control your speed. Respect others on the mountain, especially in high-traffic areas where trails are merging.

KNOW THE CODE. IT'S YOUR RESPONSIBILITY.
This is a partial list. Be safety conscious.

the pace picked up, Luke was always the last one down. Kevin had not yet had the opportunity to watch Luke as closely as he wanted, and he had a gut feeling that Luke might need more coaching before tackling the toughest trail on the mountain. "How about going to Pot O' Gold first? Then we can see how the conditions will be and whether it's a good day to try Jaws."

This response bought Kevin more time with the group before making a decision that could result in injury.

Remember that you're in charge—use your discretion to make the kinds of decisions that are in the best interest of the group.

Emotional State

Your students may be physically capable of negotiating more difficult terrain, but if they are hesitant or frightened by your choice of slope, their ability to learn and improve will be compromised. Instead of shocking them with too much challenge all at once, create a plan that will gradually ease them into more and more challenge. This can be accomplished by staying on comfortable slopes while increasing the speed or creating a more difficult task that will simulate the conditions of the desired terrain.

Jenna was a fairly accomplished snowboarder. However, when she approached more challenging terrain, she would freeze up, perform poorly, and scare herself in the process. Jenna's coach, Stacey, decided to build up Jenna's confidence by providing her with experiences that she could handle and that would show her she really was capable of riding more difficult terrain.

Stacey began the process by taking Jenna to a comfortable slope and asking her to follow in her track and to stay a certain distance behind her, getting neither closer nor farther away. Stacey then rode at a moderate speed to allow Jenna to practice. When Stacey was satisfied that Jenna had been successful, she picked up the pace. Next, Stacey varied the turn shape and made sudden turns that Jenna would have to follow. Then, Stacey found short, steeper spots on the trail. She asked Jenna to perform difficult tasks in that spot and to compare how the movements felt with the previous exercises.

Finally, Jenna was not only ready to tackle the steep trails, she was anxious to get going. Stacey's job didn't stop there. When they arrived at the top of the slope, Stacey was alert to Jenna's body language and demeanor. Fear can reestablish itself at any time, and Jenna wanted to be ready. After determining that Jenna was excited and nervous, but not frozen, Stacey reminded Jenna of the accomplishments thus far. Then, she asked Jenna what she would feel most comfortable with—following, or picking her own path.

Stacey helped Jenna choose tactics that would make the run as easy as possible ("Stay to the right of the slope, the snow is better, and there is less traffic"). Stacey stayed close to Jenna to provide moral support and encouragement. Jenna was also careful to point out that the task for the run was to complete the trail and get used to the pitch; they'd worry about technique later. Experiencing the slope itself would be a victory. And it was!

BRIAN W. ROBB

PHOTO 6.1 Help students learn to choose the right terrain for their ability level.

The success of a given task or learning activity is critically dependent on the appropriateness of the selected terrain (photo 6.1). Any task designed to have students focus inward on body and snow tool will be unsuccessful if the terrain is so challenging that the student must focus on external stimuli such as weather, terrain, and snow conditions.

Carey had a group of intermediate adults who wanted to learn how to maintain control on steep slopes. He noticed that they needed to become more aware of moving for balance and decided to do some slow-motion drills, but he kept them on the same busy slope as for the initial evaluation. As they began the drills, some of the students were so focused on controlling their speed that they forgot to pay attention to other traffic. Other students were so distracted by the traffic that they couldn't concentrate on the exercise. Carey recognized the problem before the group got too far and took them to an easier, less crowded slope so they could focus on their movements.

Slope or Trail Conditions

Whenever possible, determine the conditions on a given run before venturing there with students. Trail reports and the personal experience of yourself or other pros are the best tools. A perfect spot for coaching beginner bumps may become the worst spot if a snowmaking gun has failed or the slope is too crowded. Sideslipping exercises will be useless in powder, hop turns will be less successful on steep bump runs, and so forth.

Don't give in to the temptation to "reward" students for a good day of progress by taking them on a slope that's too difficult—too icy, too bumped-out, or too much powder or crud—for their ability. This can cause students to revert to survival mode and actually regress, ending the lesson on a negative note. Ending on a positive note by using the final run of the session as a confidence builder will give your students psychological momentum for their next outing.

PACING

Most people have a regular energy flow that roughly corresponds with the timing of meals. Typically, students warm up in the morning, reach their peak around mid-morning, and start losing energy shortly before lunch. After lunch, the group may be slow to warm up as their food is digested, have an energy peak at mid-afternoon, and begin to slow down at the end of the day. It usually is best not to have students head for the hardest run at the end of the day.

Take these natural energy cycles into account when planning the day's activities in terms of intensity, terrain, and timing of breaks.

PREPAREDNESS

An ounce of prevention is worth a pound of cure. Your best opportunity to minimize risk for yourself and your group is to check their preparedness before hitting the slopes. No matter the ability level or experience of the class, try to assess their gear and clothing every time, every lesson, every day. As you begin to discover who your students are, you can ask simple questions about their equipment and clothing:

"Serge, I heard you say that those are new boots. Did you have your bindings adjusted to them?"

Questions regarding experience in other sports can give you an idea of the fitness levels of those in your care. If you have students who rarely venture outside the office, you will need to pace the lesson differently than if they are athletes.

"Charlene, since you haven't ridden your board yet this season, let's warm up slowly and pay attention to how you feel before we head for the slopes you were riding last year."

Clothing plays a big role in the comfort of your students. If they are not prepared with proper eye wear, adequate covering for hands and ears, enough layers to keep them warm at the top of the mountain, or a wind or water shell as conditions dictate, explain the risks and offer possible solutions. The consequences of not doing so could range from interference with a student's ability to focus on learning, to frostbite!

When the risk is explained to students, they usually are happy to get the required items. If cost or availability are issues, try to find alternatives so the day and the lesson are not lost. Many resorts keep unclaimed items in lost and found for these emergencies.

Exposure to Ultraviolet Radiation

Sunshine provides the blue skies and bright snow that make the alpine environment such a phenomenal place, but the sun's ultraviolet rays present risk to snowsports participants. We are at increased risk of skin damage and, potentially, skin cancer in the alpine environment due to high elevation and the reflectivity of snow. For every 1,000 feet of elevation gain, the sun's ultraviolet rays increase 5 to 6 percent.

Exposure to UV radiation is exacerbated on snow (or water), because our skin receives sunlight both directly (from the sky) and indirectly (as reflection). These conditions also put unprotected eyes at risk.

Educate your students about the importance of protecting themselves from sun-related injury by wearing sunscreen and UV-reducing goggles or sunglasses, and remind them to occasionally reapply during the lesson—especially if at higher elevations or later in the season. It's a good idea to carry a small amount of waterproof sunscreen with you so that you can share with any students who have failed to provide their own.

Localized Skin Injuries from Cold

Temperatures and windchill factors in the winter environment can be extremely low, posing physical risk of injury to exposed tissues. When human tissues freeze, ice crystals actually form, leading to irreversible blockage of small blood vessels. Ironically, frozen skin tissue is damaged similar to a burn.

The mildest form of cold injury—frostnip—tends to occur on body surfaces farthest from the core: the ears, nose, cheeks, hands, and feet. Frostnip is characterized by pain and blanching (whiteness) of the skin. It is possible to be unaware of this process, and children in particular should be watched closely. When whiteness is noticed, take immediate steps to warm the area of skin to prevent frostbite, a more dangerous condition.

Immersion foot syndrome is a serious cold injury in which the extremity is kept cold and wet for long periods but not frozen. Although not as serious as frostbite, this condition can be painful and cause soft-tissue damage.

Frostbite occurs when tissue actually freezes, which can cause destruction of the skin and underlying muscle. If frostbite is detected, avoid rapid warming, refreezing, or physical pressure on the damaged tissue. Protect the affected area from further exposure and get the injured person to a medical facility for treatment and further evaluation. Treatment consists of slow, progressive warming of the affected area followed by long-term follow-up care.

To help your students avoid these problems, educate them about the effects of these potentially serious conditions and show them how to prevent injury with proper clothing and attention to conditions. Explain the importance of preparing for the alpine environment by dressing in layers of lightweight, absorbent, breathable, wind and waterproof clothing. Hats, neck gaiters, facemasks, and goggles can become survival gear in extreme weather. Let the students know that warm, sunny valleys can turn to cold, windy peaks in the time it takes to ride a lift. Without experience, it is easy to misjudge the changes in weather that are possible with just a relatively small amount of increase in elevation.

In addition to educating students about proper attire for extreme weather, it also is appropriate to discourage the use of tobacco and alcohol, both of which tend to constrict near-surface blood vessels and impede blood circulation to the skin. Take frequent breaks to get warm and encourage a hot beverage to raise core body temperature. When a lodge or other facility is not nearby, heat-generating activities such as bouncing in place may help get the blood flowing—but be careful to avoid sweating, which can make matters worse.

Hypothermia

Hypothermia occurs when the core body temperature falls below 95°F. Normal body temperature is approximately 98.6°F, and a core temperature below 91°F usually results in confusion and loss of consciousness. Core temperatures below 86°F can cause potentially fatal heart arrhythmia. Heat loss in the alpine environment occurs from:

- **Convection**
  Movement of air across the body.
- **Conduction**
  Contact with a cold surface, including snow.
- **Radiation**
  Movement of heat from the body toward cold surfaces not being touched.

- **Evaporation**
  Loss of heat during the process by which perspiration moves from the liquid state to the gaseous state.

The body regulates heat loss by restricting blood flow to the skin by shunting blood to internal organs. Early symptoms of temperature loss include shivering and slow response to stimuli. Bring your group inside quickly if you notice these changes.

Dehydration

Most people associate dehydration with summer activities such as running and cycling. Winter sports also require physical exertion and loss of moisture due to perspiration and rapid, deep breathing. Even in cooler temperatures, it is possible to lose 1 to 3 quarts of water per hour during high-intensity nordic skiing.

Spring in the mountains can bring warm temperatures and snow conditions that require hard work. Sudden wind gusts, increasing cloud cover, or deepening shade as the sun gets lower in the sky can quickly turn a warm, sweaty day into a cold, shivering one.

The effects of even mild dehydration include a slight headache, decreased coordination, fatigue, and impairment of judgment—not a good combination on the side of a mountain.

Our bodies don't always do a perfect job of letting us know when we are getting dehydrated. It is possible to lose fluid so quickly that the normal thirst mechanism is overwhelmed. Continually remind your students to drink water before they feel thirsty. Additionally, alcohol and caffeine are diuretics that contribute to depletion of the body's water supply and should be avoided if possible, especially during periods of exertion. Perhaps the most common symptom, the slight headache, is ignored or attributed to something else.

Remind your students that headaches can be a warning sign for dehydration and that intake of fluids should provide relief before the condition worsens.

Altitude

Ascending to an elevation 6,000 feet or more above sea level can cause physical changes in the body. While most eastern resorts are below this level, many western resorts have terrain that is significantly higher—over 12,000 feet. For this reason, it is important to understand the possible affects of altitudes on the human body and to be prepared to educate your students and cope with symptoms.

Acute mountain sickness (AMS) can affect anyone. Within 8 to 24 hours of travel to elevations above 6,000 feet, an individual who is not acclimatized may experience fatigue, headache, insomnia, and shortness of breath. At higher elevations, swelling of the brain (cerebral edema) can occur and may be life-threatening.

Rapid descent to a lower elevation at the earliest sign of mountain sickness will prevent these serious conditions from developing. Recognizing the early signs may be difficult. Some may think they are merely tired or had a bit too much to drink the night before. As a pro, you should be alert for the signs of AMS, particularly if you work at a high-elevation resort, and take steps to get severely affected persons off the mountain and to a

medical facility as quickly as possible. The physician may even recommend transportation of the person from the resort to a much lower elevation, where the reversal of symptoms can be rapid and dramatic.

Students from low-elevation areas, regardless of ability, should be eased into the higher elevation environment and reminded to drink lots of water.

AVALANCHES

The pull of fresh snow in the mountains is strong for pros and guests alike. Nothing is quite like turn after turn in bottomless powder. Yet, avalanches cause many needless deaths each year (photo 6.2). Twenty-one fatalities from avalanche occurred in 1999–2000 in the U.S. alone, and

PHOTO 6.2 Avalanche awareness is an imperative in the backcountry.

CORBIS

272 fatalities have occurred since 1985. Of these deaths, only three were in-bounds at a resort.

An avalanche is a mass of snow sliding down the mountainside. It can also be called a snowslide. The Colorado Avalanche Information Center (CAIC) lists four ingredients of an avalanche:

- A steep slope
- Snow cover
- A weak layer in the snow cover
- A trigger

Avalanches are most likely to occur after major snowstorms or during periods of thaw. The vast majority of avalanches occur on slopes steeper than 20° to 25°, and the most common slope angle for avalanches is 30° to 45°. Avalanches are actually less common on steeper slopes because the snow tends to break loose before it can reach critical depths. Avalanches occur most frequently above timberline on slopes that face away from the prevailing winds, where snow collects. They can also occur below timberline in gullies, road cuts, and small openings in the forest.

Although you cannot eliminate avalanche risk entirely, you can take measures to minimize it. These include the following:

- Climb, descend, or cross avalanche areas one at a time.
- Cross at the very bottom or top if possible.
- Move along the edge of a slope rather than the center.
- Carry and understand how to use avalanche rescue gear.

The moral of the story is that avalanches are not to be taken lightly. If you take people into the backcountry, it is imperative that you learn all you can about the dangers of avalanches and how to minimize your risk.

PHOTO 6.3 Learning to use the chairlift is as important as learning any other snowsports skill.

COACHING PROPER LIFT PROCEDURES

For many beginners, getting on and off a lift will be one of their most challenging tasks. Keep yourself well versed in the lift loading and unloading procedures and policies at your resort (photo 6.3).

The following general guidelines for use of chairlifts can be adapted for other lifts as well. Be sure to follow any and all written instructions for different lifts at your resort. Students should be told to...

- Advance to the "wait here" board or sign.
- Wait for the signal from the operator.
- Advance to the loading point.
- Skiers hold the poles in the hand away from center of the chair (outside hand when loading on inside of chair, inside hand when loading on outside of chair).
- Look over the shoulder for an oncoming chair.
- Allow the chair to touch the back of the knees before sitting.

- Keep the skis or snowboard pointed straight forward when sitting down on the chair.
- Sit back and lower the restraint bar (if the chair is so equipped).

Before taking students to the lift for their first ride up, spend time discussing how to unload:

- Raise the restraint bar well before reaching the top of the lift (watch for instructional signs, such as "raise restraint bar here").
- Skiers place equal pressure on the skis as they contact the exit platform.
- Snowboarders place the rear foot on the stomp pad as the board contacts the platform.
- Push down on the chair with the free arm.
- Rise off the chair as the platform begins to slope away.
- Glide to the end of the runout and then move to the side.
- If unable to dismount, keep skis or snowboard down and hit the stop wand (guests in this situation often raise their feet to avoid hitting the wand).

Perhaps most important, students should be reminded to never jump from the lift, even if it stops running. In the very rare need to evacuate the lift, it is important to wait for instructions and assistance from the ski patrol.

There's a lot to learn about loading and unloading a lift. Have beginners, especially children, repeat what they are going to do when getting on and off the lift. Remind children to have back-to-back and bottom-to-bottom contact with the chair.

COPING WITH ACCIDENTS AND INJURIES

Despite our best efforts, occasional accidents are inevitable, and you may be the first person in a position of authority to arrive on an accident scene. It is important to know what to do. Policies and procedures vary among resorts, so confirm this information with your individual resort policy.

If an injury happens in your session, do all you can to make the injured comfortable and warm without moving them or removing equipment. Follow your resort's procedures for notifying the ski patrol, and reassure the injured person that you have done so. Be sure to give specifics about location so rescue can happen quickly.

Ask other students in your group to cross skis or snowboards in the trail above the scene and otherwise warn oncoming traffic of the obstruction in the slope. Keep the rest of your group occupied with helping, while ensuring that they do not put themselves at risk by standing in traffic, etc. If your students are children, recruit another adult staff member (if possible) to bring the rest of your group to the children's center and notify your supervisor.

Be sure you and the resort have the names and addresses of group members who witnessed the accident, as well as those of people you recruited to help. In this way, the resort can follow up with thanks. After the injured person has been removed from the slope, resume your normal activities and don't discuss the incident with anyone but your immediate supervisor. All other procedures are resort-specific.

Sometimes, small things occur that do not require actual rescue. These can include scrapes, bumps, and tricky falls that the student recovers from, yet you are left with an uncertain feeling about the outcome. Discuss any small incident such as this with a supervisor and document it as completely as possible. In this way, if something should happen later, the resort has a record. Examples include a parent returning the next day and asking about a bruise that appeared on a child's leg that morning, or someone deciding that he needed medical attention days or weeks following the lesson.

Finally, be sure to learn from the event itself. What will the experience help you to do differently or understand better? While accidents are just that, they always provide some hidden nugget of wisdom.

SUMMARY – YOUR ROLE IN MANAGING RISK

The teacher's role in managing risk can be summed up by the following:

- Advise students that mountain sports are inherently risky and that following Your Responsibility Code reduces risk.
- Reinforce "The Code" throughout the lesson.
- Conduct sessions in appropriate areas and on suitable terrain.
- Educate students about equipment, clothing, and fitness.
- Be alert to changing weather and conditions.
- Encourage the use of proper lift procedures.
- Follow appropriate accident procedures.

Sharing the Mountain Environment

"Be ready to answer to your fellow man for the trail you leave behind. The last steps depend on the first... the first step depends on the last."
— HERMAN MELVILLE

According to current market research, two of the main reasons people visit resorts are to escape their daily routines and experience the mountains (fig. 6.2). Yet, the "mountain experience" can be startlingly different

FIGURE 6.2 Make an effort to share your knowledge of the mountain environment with guests.

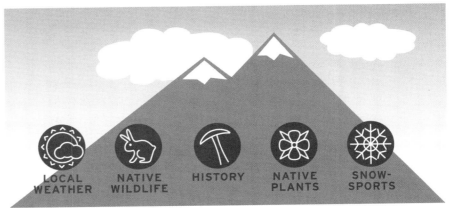

LOCAL WEATHER   NATIVE WILDLIFE   HISTORY   NATIVE PLANTS   SNOW-SPORTS

Fun + Awareness = Appreciation

from one area of the country to the next (photo 6.4). Aside from the obvious size and location of mountain resorts are differences in type and kind of services. Some resorts focus on providing luxury, while others are more rustic and provide less "padding" between the customers and nature.

Despite the obvious differences are some things that all resorts have in common:

- Some sort of history and lore of the resort and surrounding area.
- Local trends in weather and snow conditions.
- Native plants and wildlife.

While it is not a requirement that snowsports professionals also be historians or meteorologists or naturalists, it may help you to know enough to share some basic facts or answer frequently asked questions. You may find the information to be a good icebreaker on a long chair lift ride. Your guests will appreciate your knowledge of the area and will feel that they have had a richer experience than they expected.

HISTORY

Many resorts have a rich and exciting history. Some include stories of mining, logging, native Americans, and even mystery or intrigue. Children's programs are great places to use the lore of the area as themes, props, games, and teaching activities. The more stories are used, the more exciting the experience, and the more fun for you and your group. If you don't consider yourself particularly good with children, this may be just the venue to help you get started or have more fun.

PHOTO 6.4 Ski areas vary wildly from one part of the country to the next.

CLIMATE AND WEATHER

The weather is almost always a topic of conversation. "When is it going to snow again?" "Why is it always windy here?" "What's the weather going to do tomorrow?" Many of the city-dwellers you will teach spend most of their days padded from nature and have lost touch with the effects of weather on their daily lives.

Arming yourself with some local climate and folklore about weather patterns from long-time residents will help you provide some additional depth to the more typical shallow discussions. Learning to read the clouds and understanding wind patterns will also help you plan your day on the mountain to provide optimal comfort of your group.

Weather forecasts, while not always accurate, can mean the difference between a great experience and a difficult one (photo 6.5). If you are

aware of a possible front moving in that will change the wind speed and direction and cause the temperatures to drop, you can help prepare your students so they are comfortable when the changes occur.

The teenage girls showed up for Kyle's clinic with sunglasses, light windbreakers, and not a hat among them. "Hey, where are your hats?"

"They absolutely kill the hairstyle, and besides, it's really warm and sunny! We don't need them!" replied Katie, full of confidence.

"Well, I just listened to the mountain weather, and there's a storm coming in later."

"Yeah, but not until tomorrow."

"Well, they're calling for snow tomorrow, but the winds are going to pick up later today, and the clouds will cover the sun. Where we will be riding is pretty exposed."

"Oh, we hadn't thought of that."

"Hey, I have a backpack, let's put hats and extra layers in there, okay?"

Kyle got an extra tip for that one!

Remember, being prepared for weather is not just a matter of allowing your students to be comfortable so they can focus on the lesson. It could mean the difference between success or failure and could prevent injury.

WILDLIFE

Another great topic for lift rides and subject for kids groups is the local wildlife (not the bar crowd). While large animals don't normally cross the slopes at resorts during the day, one pro at a Maine resort was actually awarded a re-run in a race when a moose got in his way! Although spotting large mammals on the slopes may be rare, they are sometimes encountered while on a backcountry tour, and their tracks are often seen from the chairlift. Birds are easy to observe while riding quietly at tree-top level or having lunch on a sunny deck (photo 6.6). All of these encounters with wildlife can enliven and enrich the snowsports experience.

Knowing some basic facts about predators and prey, understanding why some species remain active in the winter while others hibernate

or migrate, and being able to identify and interpret tracks in the snow can provide great tales for children's classes and points of interest for adults as well.

PLANT LIFE

Learning to identify local forest trees provides other possibilities for education and entertainment. Many guests will be fascinated by the differences in plant life at different elevations or on different exposures (photo 6.7). Prevailing winds and continued frost damage at higher elevations can create bizarre and interesting plant shapes.

Trees are a wonderful source of visual and ecological diversity and help shape the mountain experience for snowsports participants. Unlike wildlife, trees are readily observed from lifts or while resting along the edge of a slope. What's the difference between a pine, a fir, and a spruce? Between an aspen and a birch? Why are some are slopes covered by uniform stands of a single species while others contain a variety of species and sizes? Helping to bring

PHOTO 6.6 Mountain resorts share wildlife habitat.

the forest to life for your guests will add to your credibility as a mountain guide and add to the alpine experience for yourself and your guests.

A WORD ON SUMMER ACTIVITY

Mountain ecosystems are delicate, and the short growing season provides limited time for nature to heal any wounds. Resorts once were refuges from human activity in summer, but many have become popular destinations for hiking, cycling, or other types of mountain recreation. If not carefully managed, these activities can pose a threat to the environment we love, in terms of erosion, damage to vegetation, and disturbance of wildlife.

Encourage any of your guests who plan to return to the mountains in summer to be respectful of the mountain environment and the creatures that share it with us. The easiest ways to accomplish this are to stay on designated trails, leave flowers and fruits as food for wildlife and as sources of new plants, and respect posted closures of sensitive habitats.

SUSTAINABLE SLOPES

In June 2000, the National Ski Areas Association unveiled an "Environmental Charter for Ski Areas (table 6.2)." This charter was designed to guide resorts in three categories:

1. **Planning and Design**
   To engage surrounding communities and interest groups in a dialogue on development plans.
2. **Operations**
   To conserve natural resources in such areas as water, energy, waste management, fish and wildlife, forest and vegetative management, wetlands and riparian areas, air quality and visual quality.
3. **Education and Outreach**
   To use the natural surroundings as a means of increasing environmental awareness and enhancing the relationship between resorts and other stakeholders.

The Charter outlines "best management practices" for resorts and provides options to reach the goals stated. Resorts that endorse the Charter (over 165 resorts nationwide had done so as of this writing) will assess current practices and begin making alterations. Further, they agree to report annually on their progress. This may involve participation by outside organizations that signed on as "partners" to provide technical and financial assistance.

Some of the ski resort partners include the Mountain Institute, a nonprofit organization that preserves mountain culture, lifestyle, and environment; the National Fish and Wildlife Foundation, a nonprofit organization that invests in local conservation efforts; the U.S. Forest Service, and many others. The goal is "sustainable slopes," which is good news for both the environment and the winter sports industry (see Stacy Gardner, *Bringing the Environmental Charter to Life*). The "sustainable slopes" logo is now appearing at resorts across the country, as is the Environmental Code of the Slopes.

TABLE 6.2 The Environment Charter for Ski Areas

What You Can Do

SIX STEPS TO SUSTAINABLE SLOPES

1. PACK IT IN—PACK IT OUT
   Leave nature how you found it.
2. RESPECT WILDLIFE by observing trail closures and ski area boundaries.
3. SHARE A RIDE so we can breathe fresh air and see the views.
4. BE CONSIDERATE of others' experiences and let nature's sounds prevail.
5. GET INVOLVED in your local resort or community's environmental program.
6. SPREAD THE WORD to your liftmates, friends, and family.

Professional Development

chapter 7

- Personal Mastery
- Fitness
- Equipment
- Revitalizing your career

> *"Personal excellence is a contest with yourself to draw on the natural reserves within your own mind and body, to develop your capabilities to the utmost."*
>
> — TERRY ORLICK
> IN PURSUIT OF EXCELLENCE: HOW TO WIN IN SPORT AND LIFE THROUGH MENTAL TRAINING

Your success and longevity as a snowsports instructor requires both a desire for improvement and a commitment to personal growth. The old adage, "if you're not growing, you're dying" certainly applies to our profession. Teaching is almost unique among careers in that the constant flow of new students—with new attitudes, interests, and vocabularies—can turn today's top teacher into tomorrow's dinosaur. Even if students themselves were to never change, the need to understand how continually evolving equipment affects learning and performance makes your task doubly challenging.

Effective growth in teaching any sport is a function of knowing what you want to accomplish (your vision) and developing a plan for getting there. The resources for development and improvement are many, yet you will need to seek them out. From the locker room to the board room, from the beginner hill to the extreme slopes of the highest mountain, from new participants to seasoned pros, from the revered wise ones to babes in the children's programs, you must tap the minds of guests, peers, coaches, and mentors.

Personal Mastery

"People with a high level of personal mastery live in a continual learning mode. They never arrive."
— SENGE

The term "personal mastery" refers to being the best that you can be. It is a journey, not a destination. Those committed to it learn to welcome and appreciate each step along the way. Whether you are a master teacher or a new pro, your path toward personal mastery will inevitably change and evolve with time.

GETTING STARTED

"Personal mastery is not something you possess. It is a process, a lifelong discipline. People with a high level of personal mastery are acutely aware of their ignorance, their incompetence, and their growth areas."
— SENGE

You begin the path to personal mastery by defining your vision or goal (fig. 7.1). Next, evaluate the current reality—your strengths and weaknesses relative to the vision. Then, develop a plan for getting to the ultimate goal. Having an ability to enjoy the journey despite challenges and disappointments will help you stay on target.

To succeed, your vision must be tied to your intrinsic needs and desires—your "purpose" in life. It is a fundamental part of who you are. While your vision may be chosen by following your heart, the path for getting there will require considerable help from your brain. In charting the path, be realistic about where you are now and what's required to get there. Be patient, and be prepared for occasional setbacks or detours. Learn to use both successes and failures as a catalyst to help pull you along.

For many people, the best approach for pursuing their vision is to set a series of intermediate goals or "milestones." These make the journey seem less daunting and provide opportunities to adjust your vision or path as you learn more about the sport, the profession, and yourself (fig. 7.2).

FIGURE 7.1 The quest for personal mastery is never-ending, requiring vision and the motivation, commitment, and perseverance to attain goals.

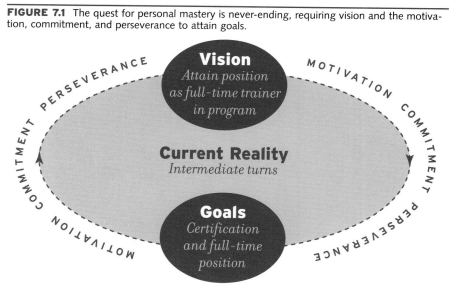

FIGURE 7.2 Technical and relationship skills work in concert to advance you toward your goal.

CARRYING THROUGH

"Start by doing what's necessary, then what's possible, and suddenly you are doing the impossible."
— SAINT FRANCIS

Once you've determined your vision, evaluated the current reality, and developed a plan for getting there, it's time to get started (fig. 7.3). Four steps will help you begin the journey:

1. **Commit**
   Be prepared to make sacrifices in terms of time, energy, and money. If these are in short supply, you may need to revise your schedule and pursue the goal over a longer period.

2. **Search**
   Discover your resources. These include trainers, supervisors, mentors, books, videos, and training sessions by PSIA-AASI or the resort. Don't forget locker-room buddies!

3. **Prioritize**
   Determine what resources and intermediate goals you need to pursue next. Ask trusted mentors for suggestions about next steps.

4. **Practice**
   Work on your weaknesses, but don't neglect your strengths. Repetition and focus are the keys, but don't lose sight of the goal or let the fun go out of the sport!

Hire a Coach

If you are truly committed to excellence in teaching and performing your sport, seek your own coach or mentor. This person will be someone to observe your performance objectively and offer feedback that will either alter or reinforce your efforts.

A coach can let you know if you are performing a movement correctly

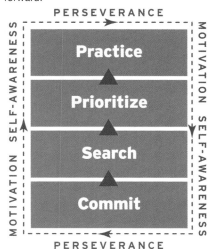

FIGURE 7.3 Establish a process for moving forward.

and help you correlate internal sensations with external results. A coach can also help you become a better teacher by helping you solve problems or just being there to listen and bounce around ideas.

For this to be successful, you must have a high level of trust in, and respect for, your coach. Otherwise, you will be tempted to resist suggestions for change that are challenging or in conflict with your own preconceptions.

Push the Envelope

Risk-taking is an important element in achieving your personal best. By pushing yourself intelligently, you can develop your potential; the improvements you will see in performance may surprise you. Intelligent risk-taking means that you are keenly aware of the possible consequences of your actions. You know your personal limits, the limits of your equipment, and the conditions of the slope and day.

Certification

PSIA-AASI has developed a member certification program that helps define and quantify the path to excellence in teaching and snowsports performance. The program includes three levels of proficiency. For a detailed listing of requirements, refer to the PSIA or AASI websites.

Certified Level I
Demonstrated ability to...
- Provide guest service.
- Manage risk.
- Present beginning level concepts and learning activities.
- Share an understanding of basic technical aspects of the sport as they pertain to beginning levels.
- Perform the sport well enough to be respected as a coach for the beginning level student.

Certified Level II

Demonstrated ability in all of the above, plus ability to...

- Present concepts and learning activities through advanced intermediate level.
- Adapt teaching to different ages and abilities.
- Make appropriate movement assessments.
- Share an understanding of technical aspects of equipment and the sport as they pertain through advanced intermediate levels.
- Perform the sport with proficiency through advanced levels on most terrain.

Certified Level III

Demonstrated ability in all of the above, plus ability to...

- Present advanced level concepts and learning activities.
- Share an understanding of technical aspects of equipment and the sport through advanced levels.

- Perform the sport with proficiency through advanced levels on all but the most extreme terrain.

PSIA-AASI also offers training for those wishing to obtain trainer and examiner status. Training and tryouts for these positions are very demanding and competitive and require full-time participation in the sport. For those who strive for still higher levels, PSIA-AASI holds tryouts every four years for the National Demonstration Teams in alpine skiing, nordic skiing, and snowboarding disciplines.

The National Demonstration Teams are an elite group who exhibit the highest standards of proficiency in their given sports. These teams travel throughout the country, providing training and inspiration to the membership of the association.

Fitness

Your fitness level will ultimately determine your ability to enjoy your sport, both as recreation and a vocation (photos 7.1 and 7.2). Young or old, new pro or old hand, your fitness level will determine your risk of injury and ability to improve performance.

A total fitness program must balance the needs for flexibility, strength, and endurance. Alpine skiing and snowboarding tend to build strength disproportionately to flexibility and endurance. Nordic enthusiasts have the benefit of building both endurance and strength. Regardless of the particular combination of snowsports, any program should be supplemented with a well-rounded conditioning program that includes flexibility training.

Basic components of a conditioning program include activities that focus on:

- Motor control, such as coordination, balance, and agility.
- Aerobic and anaerobic capacity.
- Muscular strength and endurance.
- Muscle flexibility and joint mobility.

In addition to targeting the basic elements of conditioning, you can improve specific components of performance with exercises that imitate the movement patterns of a particular activity. This is the basic principle of training known as specificity. First you have to understand the movements of your sport. In simple terms, all snowsports involve progressing down (or up) a snow-covered slope in a controlled manner. When moving down the slope, turning is used to change direction and control speed. Therefore, a fundamental objective of snowsports is to maintain balance under dynamic conditions.

Be sure to check with your doctor before beginning any new regimen—especially if you no longer think of yourself as a "young pup." An evaluation by a healthcare professional such as a physical therapist or exercise physiologist can also provide the information you need to design a personalized workout program.

Equipment

Winter sports are by nature "gear intensive." Like all sports—or other human endeavors—that represent the union of a human participant with equipment, both alpine and nordic snowsports have seen continual and at times mind-boggling advancements in equipment, boots, clothing, and accessories. This evolution has been faster for snowsports than many pursuits because of the dramatic improvement that can result form relatively minor refinements, tremendous advances in materials that are stronger but lighter, and the amount of money that snowsports enthusiasts are willing to spend to improve their performance or comfort.

For participants in any winter sport, potential questions about gear are almost endless: What is the best gear? How can I tell if it is working for me? How do I know if it fits? Is what I'm using holding me back? Will adaptations make me better?

Your students will expect you to know and understand their gear—not just if it is right for them, but how to fix it if it isn't or what to buy to make it right.

Be aware of a colossal "but" here: People who have just purchased what they thought was the cat's pajamas in gear, and who spent their life savings doing so, don't want someone (i.e., you) telling them it stinks! Find out about their equipment history; no matter how far below your standards, their new equipment may be light years ahead of what they had previously. Also, be sure to understand their needs. Someone whose goal is just to be able to make it down an intermediate slope a few times a year without falling has much different equipment needs than someone who has shown rapid improvement, is ready for the next step, and has high goals.

Jorge came to the clinic after purchasing gear from his friend. Jorge was a small man whose primary sport was rock-climbing. His friend was an ex-football player who was now immersed in snowsports and considered himself an expert. Jorge was very proud of his purchase but confessed he came to the lesson to determine why his skills seemed to regress since purchasing the new gear.

Leslie took one look and knew Jorge's problem right away. "Hey, where did you get your gear?" After a short discussion, Leslie knew that she would have to be very careful with how to proceed.

Jorge was planning to visit the mountain more often and was very committed to improvement. Leslie helped him understand that his performance regressing because his gear was meant for a bigger person, shared some possible options with him, from retrofitting the newly acquired gear with different boots, to selling the whole outfit and purchasing used equipment from a reputable dealer. She mentioned that the pro shop on the mountain had some good deals on demo equipment and took used gear in trade.

If Jorge had been satisfied with his performance and was only looking for a short-term fix, Leslie would have been less inclined to focus on the equipment. By the end of the lesson, through sensitively sharing with Jorge what would be optimal for him when the opportunity presented itself, Leslie had helped Jorge eliminate an impediment to his success—and hers.

WHAT IS OPTIMAL GEAR?

The best gear for an individual is what fits him or her and is designed for the specific use. Powder skis may not be the best choice for recreational racing. A racing snowboard wouldn't be good for a small-statured half-pipe novice. Back-country skis are a poor choice for skating, and skating skis are a poor choice for telemarking. The key is to understand what your students want to achieve, and what is available out there for them.

To increase your knowledge about equipment, start with the industry magazines that your students are likely to read. The information in these magazines is written specifically for consumers—making it relatively easy to understand, even for "non-gearheads." Reading the popular magazines will also prepare you for questions the students are likely to ask.

Next, go to your local retail shop and ask some questions. Find out how various types of equipment look, and why. Use the professionals at your favorite shop, and other teaching pros at your resort, as resources. Their experience with different brands and types of gear will arm you with stories and facts to relate to your students.

PHOTO 7.3 Try out as many different types of gear as you can.

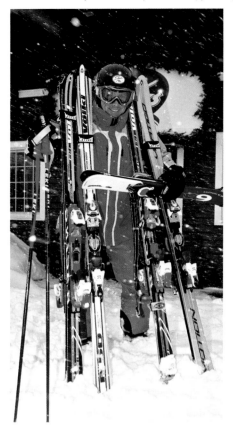

Finally, get out and try as many different kinds of gear as you can (photo 7.3). You can usually do this through consumer demo days. Often, resort retail and rental shops will let staff try different gear on a limited basis. Check your resort policy.

CUSTOMIZING YOUR GEAR

To optimize your own performance, it may be important to customize your gear rather than using it "off the rack." Everyone is built and moves a little differently, and even slight mismatches between physique and equipment can detract significantly from performance and improvement.

The first step is to check your alignment with a reputable trainer or health care professional. For example, minor differences in leg length or ankles that tend to roll inward (pronate) or outward (supinate) from the neutral position can seriously affect your ability to apply pressure precisely and consistently. Custom footbeds or boot shims can reduce or eliminate these problems.

If you've been experiencing frustrating plateaus that you can't seem to surmount regardless of study and practice, you may find that customizing your gear or making some simple modifications can get you back on track. The benefits of customized gear go beyond your own performance; they can also improve your teaching. Your students will benefit from your increased awareness of the importance of proper equipment, and your own improvement will boost your confidence and your fun meter.

For more information on specific customization for your sport, refer to your sport-specific manual.

Revitalizing Your Career

"Do not burn yourselves out. Be as I am. A reluctant enthusiast and part-time crusader. A half-hearted fanatic. Save the other half of your- selves for pleasure and adventure. It is not enough to fight for the west. It is even more important to enjoy it while you can, while it's still there. So get out there, hunt, fish, mess around with your friends, ramble out yonder and explore the forests, encounter the griz, climb a moun- tain, bag the peaks, run the rivers, breathe deep of that yet sweet and elusive air. Sit quietly for a while and contemplate the precious still- ness of the lovely, mysterious and awesome space. Enjoy yourselves. Keep your brain in your head and your head firmly attached to the body, the body active and alive. And I promise you this one sweet victory over our enemies, over those desk-bound people with their hearts in safe deposit boxes and their eyes hypnotized by their desk calcula- tors. I promise you this: You will outlive the bastards."
— Edward Abbey
   in a speech to environmentalists
   in Missoula, Montana, 1978

What is the secret of staying ener- gized about teaching your sport? How can you keep your attitude fresh and your feet fresh too? According to Parker Palmer (1998), it is important to reconnect with what sparked your desire to teach. Think about your mentors, your friends in the sport, and the sport itself. What did it have that attracted you? Did you choose it, or did it choose you? Finding something to focus your energy on can rekindle the embers of your inner fire.

"As we try to connect ourselves and our subjects with our students, we make ourselves, as well as our subjects, vulnerable to indifference, judgment, ridicule. To reduce our vulnerability, we disconnect from students, from subjects, and even from ourselves. We build a wall between inner truth and outer performance, and we play-act the teacher's part.... We distance ourselves from students and subject to minimize the danger—forgetting that distance makes life more dan- gerous still by isolating the self."
— Palmer

To avoid this disconnect, you must have realistic expectations for your- self and your students. Gradually, you will gain an understanding of the true nature of what is expected of a teacher—the challenges and the rewards, the hours, the weather, the people, the pay. The more you truly understand the job, the more likely you will be to chase opportunity rather than wait for it to chase you.

Facing reality may be your biggest challenge. After all, you're already good at your sport—very good—and you must enjoy being around people, or you wouldn't have given this pro- fession a second glance. But don't confuse facing reality with selling your students short. Expect the best from people, even when they don't come through. Recognize that even the best of intentions sometimes prove off-track and you end up hav- ing to do more than your fair share to keep things rolling. Accepting that no one is perfect (not even you), appre- ciating the effort as well as the result, and realizing that every student has something to teach as well as some- thing to learn can keep you energized through the toughest of seasons.

"In combating cynicism, it helps to know its source. Scratch the surface of most cynics and you find a frus- trated idealist—someone who made the mistake of converting his ideals into expectations. For example, many of those cynical about person- al mastery once held high ideals about people. Then they found themselves disappointed, hurt, and eventually embittered because people fell short of their ideal.... Burnout comes from causes other than simply working too hard. There are teachers, social workers, and clergy who work incredibly hard until they are 80 years old and never suffer burnout—because they have an accurate view of human nature. They don't over-romanticize people, so they don't feel the great psychological stress when people let them down."
— Senge

APPRECIATING DIVERSITY

"It is not from ourselves that we will learn to be better than we are."
— Wendell Berry

One way to stay excited about devel- oping your teaching skill is to learn about a special population or another snowsport. Diversification will pro- vide new perspectives on learning, coaching, and performance. Through diversification, you will become more valuable to your alpine, nordic, or snowboard school in addition to providing yourself with an antidote for getting stuck in a rut.

Women
Recent industry publications are targeting women as the decision- makers in the family when it comes to vacations. If mom isn't crazy about winter sports, she's not going to want to hang around for long, shopping or reading, while hubby and the kids have all the fun.

Helping make women passionate about snowsports is critical to keeping the family coming back for more.

Most programs now include clinics specifically for women. Some women feel more comfortable learning new skills with and from other women. There's a different atmosphere in a group of women than in a mixed group. In a group of women, it can be easier to ask questions and focus on learning, so progress is quicker.

It sometimes is amazing to see the support and camaraderie that women can provide in a group. The atmosphere stays just as competitive, just as intense, yet the competition is within, not between, individuals. The intensity goes toward pushing each other as far as possible without sacrificing self-worth by comparing one's own goals or progress with those of others.

Get Involved

PSIA-AASI divisions often provide special education, both through clinics for women only and in clinics to teach men how to teach women.

Children

Nationally, children represent 50 to 60 percent of all lessons taught. What better place to leave a legacy than with a group of kids who come back year after year and ask specifically for you? Children are exciting to coach: they are energetic, learn quickly, and push themselves willingly.

The main challenge in teaching children is to keep them safe and learning while having more fun than they, or you, dreamed possible. This can be the easiest task for you on some days, and the most difficult on others.

The best thing about coaching children is that they have a unique way of reminding you of why you came to the mountains in the first place. If it isn't fun, it isn't worth doing. This forces the teacher to connect the drills and teaching activities with the fun they were designed to produce... something we all lose sight of from time to time.

Learning to tap into your imagination to capture the attention of a group of young children will help you bring the same creativity to all aspects of your coaching.

What you need to know:

- How to motivate children.
- Ages and stages of development.
- Physical capabilities for different age groups.
- Recognizing limitations in equipment.
- How to involve parents in the process.

Get Involved

All PSIA-AASI divisions offer clinics geared toward teaching children. Most divisions now offer a "Children's Accreditation" program and give special recognition for children's educators.

Seniors

Everyone's getting older. It's inevitable. Yet, growth in snowsports participation among seniors is disproportionately small compared to the population at large. Aging snowsports enthusiasts are heading to other activities such as golf at a rapid and, from some perspectives, alarming rate. Happily, the ones who stay are realizing that they can continue to enjoy the mountain environment far into their later years.

Seniors groups are springing up all over the country. With names like "Silver Wings" and "Prime Time," the focus is on enjoying the thrill of winter sports and the mountain environment. Their purpose also includes a social component as they look for ways to meet and interact with others now that they don't have jobs to go to and their children have reached adulthood and are busy with their own lives and families.

While elders are less energetic and slower at showing improvement than younger groups, teaching them has its own rewards. These are people who have learned to savor life, to appreciate a gorgeous day and beautiful scenery, to revel in seemingly minor accomplishments, to draw from the energy of their younger instructor—and to make every run count.

PSIA-AASI members age too. As we age, we discover tricks to help us "keep up" longer. Sharing these insights with other aging participants can be gratifying and exciting both for older professionals and for younger ones seeking wisdom from their senior peers and mentors.

Get Involved

PSIA-AASI divisions are beginning to offer clinics just for the older set and educating their teaching staff on the special needs of this group.

Adaptive

For any winter sport professional who wants to gain a sense of what really matters, coaching in an adaptive program may fill the bill (photo 7.4). To coach students with special physical or mental needs, a pro must look for what each student can do, instead of what he or she can't. This often is a monumental challenge that forces you to change your own definition of success.

Adaptive teaching doesn't mean lowering expectations, but realizing that success has many facets and that finding a path to success for each student is the ultimate challenge. Helping someone with one leg learn to be independent with outriggers, or a paraplegic learn to negotiate the mountain on a sled, can open up a whole new world of possibilities for growth and appreciation of the sport—and of life—for you as well as the student.

Get Involved

PSIA-AASI offers clinics and a track of certification that specializes in adaptive education. A variety of symposia and national events are available across the country to help teach teachers and sponsor adaptive programs.

Cross-Discipline

Another way to rejuvenate yourself and your career is to learn a new snowsport. Starting anew is a wonderful way for teachers to not only recapture the spirit of learning but to help remember what it's like to feel awkward and helpless. Nothing will help you appreciate the challenges your students are facing more than to put yourself in the same situation. Through this experience comes a realization that a good experience from a gifted teacher can mean the difference between sticking with it or quitting.

As I crossed the slope, I was suddenly all too aware of the nearness of the trees and the speed at which they were approaching. "Maggie, let go of the edge and turn!", I heard from the poor soul trying to coach me. He was very patient, but he didn't know that the trees were coming at me at such an alarming rate. How could I possibly remember how to get off an edge with that advancing army?

In a panic, I reached for the inviting padding of the snow and embraced it for all I was worth. It had to be softer than trees. As I lay on the ground and my patient coach hiked up to me, I pondered my physical and mental state. Could it be that all those beginners I had coached over the years had felt this way? Was it even remotely possible that they, too, had felt the bunny hill closely resembled Mount Everest?

As I regained my composure, I decided to apprise my coach of my mental state—although admitting it was humbling—and help him figure out how to get past it. I wasn't going to decide against the sport; I was going to get good at it so I could help others to stick with it too.

Learning a new sport at your home resort is a great way to get peer coaching. It can provide both learning and coaching experiences for both parties if one focuses on coaching and the other on the sport. Pick a time when burnout may be close, and then go learn something new from a friend on the staff. Be prepared for some laughs and for a fresh reminder of why your guests come to the mountain.

Get Involved

If you are past the beginner stage in your second snowsport, look for certification opportunities through your PSIA-AASI division. Pursuing certification in another discipline can strengthen your coaching abilities while providing opportunities for you to stay fresh, get a change of scenery, and improve your career potential.

A FINAL THOUGHT ON RENEWAL

"Our past is not our potential. In any hour, with all the stubborn teachers and healers of history who called us to our best selves, we can liberate the future. You are not just you. You are a seed, a silent promise. You are the conspiracy."
— MARILYN FERGUSON
  FUTURIST

This book identifies the tools you need to create successful learning experiences for guests and sets forth a philosophy to guide your implementation of those teaching skills and abilities. As an instructor you must use everything within your power to create adventure, learning, and fun on the mountain—for your students and yourself.

Continue to broaden your knowledge of the core concepts of teaching, and renew your commitment to share the love of snowsports with others. With that objective in your mind and that passion in your heart, you will always be able to handle the most challenging teaching experiences as masterfully as you make turns on the mountain.

References

BIBLIOGRAPHY

AASI (American Association of Snowboard Instructors) 1998. *Snowboard Manual.* Lakewood, CO.

Abraham, H. 1983. *Skiing Right.* Johnson Books, Boulder, CO.

Allen, J. 1987. *Teaching and Technique: A History of American Ski Instruction.* PSIA-E Educational Foundation, Latham, NY.

Bach, R. 1989. *Illusions: The Adventures of a Reluctant Messiah.* Dell, New York, NY.

Birren, J., and K. Schaie, eds. 1996. *Handbook of Psychology and Aging.*

Blake, R., and J. Mouton 1964. *The Managerial Grid.* Gulf Publishing, Houston.

Blakeslee, M. 2002. *In the Yikes! Zone: A Conversation with Fear.* Penguin Putnam, New York, NY.

Bloom, B., M. Englehart, E. Furst, W. Hill, and D. Krathwohl 1956. *Taxonomy of Educational Objectives.* McKay, New York, NY.

Brown, J. and C. Moffett 1999. *The Hero's Journey.* Association for Supervision and Curriculum Development, Alexandria, VA.

Carbone, C. 1996. *Women Ski.* World Leisure Corporation, Boston, MA.

Fredston, J. and D. Fesler 1988. *Snow Sense: A Guide to Evaluation Snow Avalanche Hazard.* Alaska Mountain Safety Center, Inc., Anchorage, AK.

Gallwey, T. and R. Kriegel 1997. *Inner Skiing.* Random House, New York, NY.

Gardner, H. 1985. *Frames of Mind.* BasicBooks/ Harper-Collins Publishers, USA.

Gardner, S. 2000. *Bringing the Environmental Charter to Life.* NSAA Journal, volume 8, number 4 (August-September). National Ski Areas Association, Lakewood, CO.

Gordon, T. 1975. *Parent Effectiveness Training.* Plume, New York, NY.

Hannaford, C. 1995. *Smart Moves.* Great Ocean Publishers, Arlington, VA.

Jensen, E. 1995. *Super Teaching.* Turning Point Publishing, Del Mar, CA.

Joyce, E. and M. Loring 1997. *The Perfect Turn.* The American Skiing Company, Bethel, ME.

Kiersey, D. and M. Bates 1984. *Please Understand Me.* Prometheus Nemesis Book Company, Del Mar, CA.

Kolesnik, W. 1976. *Learning: Educational Applications.* Allyn and Bacon, Inc., Boston, MA.

Lebedun, J. 1998 *Managing Work Place Conflict.* American Media Publishing, West Des Moines, IA.

Loring, M. 2000. *Skiing: A Woman's Guide.* Ragged Mountain Press/ McGraw-Hill, Camden, ME.

Mackenzie, M. 1993. *Skiing The Mind Game.* Dell, New York, NY.

MacNeil, D. 1979. *Customer Service Excellence.* Mirrow Press, Burr Ridge, IL.

Maslow, A. 1956. *Motivation and Personality.* Harper and Rowe, New York, NY.

McCarthy, B. 1996. *About Learning,* Inc., Wauconda, IL.

Media Partners Corporation 1998. *The Unified Team.* Seattle, WA.

Millman, D. 1979. *The Warrior Athlete: Body, Mind, and Spirit.* Stillpoint Publishing, Walpole, NH.

Nelson, M. 1997. *Strong Women Stay Young.* Bantam Books, New York, NY.

Orlick, T. 1990. *In Pursuit of Excellence: How to Win in Sport and Life Through Mental Training.* Leisure Press, Champaign, IL.

Palmer, P. 1998. *The Courage To Teach.* Jossey-Bass Inc., San Francisco, CA.

Phillips, B. 1993. *Phillips' Book of Great Thoughts and Funny Sayings.* Tyndale House Publishing, Inc., Wheaton, IL.

Post Foster, E. 1995. *Technical Skills for Alpine Skiing.* Turning Point Ski Foundation, Edwards, CO.

PSIA (Professional Ski Instructors of America) 1998. *Professional Development Portfolio.* Lakewood, CO.

PSIA 1997. *Children's Instruction Manual.* Lakewood, CO.

PSIA 1997. *Adaptive Manual.* Lakewood, CO.

PSIA 1996. *Alpine Manual.* Lakewood, CO.

PSIA 1995. *Nordic Skiing.* Lakewood, CO.

PSIA 1994. *Children's Development.* Lakewood, CO.

Rohnke, K. 1984. *Silver Bullets.* Adventure Publication of the Kendall/Hunt Publishing Company. Dubuque, IA.

Rosenthal, R., and L. Jacobsen. 1968. *Pygmalion in the Classroom.* Rinehart and Winston, New York, NY.

Schoel, J., D. Prouty, and P. Radcliffe, P. 1988. *Islands of Healing: A Guide to Adventure Based Counseling.* Project Adventure, Inc., Hamilton, MA.

Senge, P. 1990. *The Fifth Discipline: The Art and Practice of The Learning Organization.* Doubleday, New York, NY.

Silberman, M. 2000. *Peoplesmart.* Berrett-Koehler Publishers, Inc., San Francisco, CA.

Thomas, K. and M. Dunnette, ed. 1976. *The Handbook of Industrial and Organizational Psychology.* Rand McNally, Chicago.

Thomas, K. and R. Kilmann 1996. *Thomas-Kilmann Conflict Mode Instrument.* Xicom, Tuxedo, NY.

Wheatley, M. and Kellner-Rogers 1999. *A Simpler Way.* Berrett-Koehler Publishers, San Francisco, CA.

Wheatley, M. 1999. *Leadership and the New Sciences.* Berrett-Koehler Publishers, San Francisco, CA.

WEBSITES

www.aasi.org
American Association of Snowboard Instructors

www.agenet.com
Information about seniors and children

www.avalanche.org
Westside Avalanche Network

www.gorp.com
Covers a variety of mountain topics, including the mountain environment

www.howtolearn.com
The Center for New Discoveries in Learning

www.mbti.com
Meyers-Briggs site for purchasing inventories (e.g., Meyers-Briggs Type Indicator) and support materials. Also has some career tips.

www.nsaa.org
National Ski Areas Association

www.nsp.org
National Ski Patrol

www.psia.org
Professional Ski Instructors of America

www.skinet.com
The "skier's marketplace for ideas and commerce"

www.snowlink.com
SnowSports Industries America

www.takeace.com
An online inventory that compares you with world class athletes and gives you concrete areas in which work on your performance. Testing fee required.

www.twsnow.com
Snowboarding-Online.com

ONLINE APPENDIX

Go to the home page of PSIA (www.psia.org) or AASI (www.aasi.org) to find material that supports this book. Information housed in this site includes evolutionary teaching concepts of PSIA-AASI, samples of mental models, archived articles from *The Professional Skier* and *The Pro Rider,* and links to various snowsport websites.

Glossary

abdominal muscles
The muscles covering that part of the body between the chest and the pelvis and enclosing the stomach, intestines, liver, spleen, and pancreas.

acute mountain sickness (AMS)
A physical condition that may occur at altitudes above 6,000 feet, AMS is caused by lack of oxygen, which injures body cells directly because it interferes with oxygen-requiring chemical reactions. AMS also injures the body cells indirectly because of the changes it causes in the circulatory, respiratory, and nervous systems. Symptoms include fatigue, weakness, headache, loss of appetite, nausea, vomiting, and shortness of breath on exertion.

adaptive
Programs or lessons tailored to the individual needs of skiers or riders requiring specialized equipment or teaching techniques. Adaptive skiers or riders may have cognitive, developmental, or physical disabilities.

aerobic exercise
Increased exertion under oxygenated conditions, as opposed to anaerobic (without oxygen) exercise. The intensity of aerobic exercise allows it to be performed for a sustained period of time. Examples are running, swimming, and nordic track skiing.

affective domain
The learning domain related to feelings, emotions, values, spirituality, and the appreciation of beauty, such as in art or wildlife. Learning a sport can create growth in the affective domain. See also *cognitive domain* and *sensorimotor domain.*

alignment
The positioning of the body so that forces derived from the interaction of the skis on the snow pass through the body's center of mass to produce the intended movement. This is optimized when the snow tool and boots are selected and/or modified to either complement or correct body movement to enhance strength and predictability of movement.

alpine skiing
Term used to distinguish downhill skiing from its nordic counterpart.

American Teaching System (ATS)
The methods, models, and philosophy of teaching snowsports as collected, developed, and disseminated by PSIA and AASI.

anaerobic exercise
Exercise in which energy is released without the use of oxygen. The body releases this type of energy via a phosphate energy-delivery system that is later replenished by oxygen. Anaerobic activities that require short bursts of energy include skiing or riding in demanding conditions such as moguls or race courses.

anatomy
The science of bodily structure.

anterior cruciate ligament (ACL)
The knee ligament that connects the femur (thigh bone) with the tibia (shin bone) and prevents the forward movement of the tibia on the femur. The posterior cruciate ligament prevents backward movements of the tibia on the femur.

assessing
The process of evaluating student characteristics to determine how to structure individualized, effective lessons.

auditory learners
They respond well to verbal descriptions of movements to be performed and generally prefer to talk about their experiences.

balancing movements
Muscular actions to maintain equilibrium, or the desired alignment, on skis or snowboard. These movements are usually divided into two categories: (1) actions that affect fore-and-aft balance and (2) actions that affect lateral balance.

ball-and-socket joint
A joint in which a knob-like part of one bone fits into a socket of another, allowing rotation as well as flexion and extension. The hip and shoulder joints are ball-and-socket joints.

bindings
Devices that attach skis or a snowboard to the boots.

biomechanics
Field of study applying the principles of mechanics to the study of animate movement.

center of gravity
Essentially the same location as the skier's or rider's center of mass.

center of mass (CM)
The point at which the entire mass of the body may be considered to be concentrated. If the body is viewed as made up of many small elements of mass, the average location of these elemental masses is the center of mass. The CM location changes as body position changes and may even be located outside the body.

closed question
A question that elicits a limited response. "Are your edges sharp?" is a closed question. See also *generative question* and *open question.*

cognitive domain
The learning domain related to thinking, analyzing, and speaking. See also *affective domain* and *sensorimotor domain.*

concentric contraction
Muscle contraction involving shortening of a muscle. See also *eccentric contraction* and *isometric contraction.*

concrete operations stage
The developmental stage that is characterized by the ability to differentiate appearance from reality.

customer service
Providing a service or product in a manner that places great value on customer satisfaction. Customer service touches all aspects of resort operations. The instructor is a conduit to the customer's overall enjoyment of the mountain experience.

demonstration
Performing a task or exercise as an example for students. Usually involves highlighting particular movements so that the students can readily see them.

drills
Repeating a task or exercise to attain a desired performance objective or retain knowledge.

eccentric contraction
Muscle contraction involving lengthening of a muscle while developing tension. Also known as negative contraction. See also *concentric contraction* and *isometric contraction.*

edging
Movements that increase or decrease edge angles.

efficiency
The expenditure of only that amount of energy required to accomplish a given task. Efficiency is the ratio of the skier's or rider's input energy to the desired output movement. High efficiency implies achieving the desired movement with a minimum input of energy under a given set of conditions.

elementary stage
The second stage of coordination development, in which spatial awareness is gained, and movement around objects becomes more refined.

eversion
Movement of a body part outward, such as a lateral movement of the sole of the foot. See also *inversion*.

experiential learning
Learning through experience. Instructors create situations through use of terrain or task for students, enabling them to learn first-hand how to apply knowledge presented during the lesson.

extension
Any movement that increases the angle at a joint. At times the skier or rider extends the knee, hip, and ankle joints simultaneously. See also *flexion*.

extensors
Muscles that enable extension at a joint. For example, the hip muscles act to extend the thigh away from the abdomen, and the trunk muscles cause the spine to arch backward.

feedback
Information students receive about their performance that helps clarify what action they need to take to achieve a desired result. Feedback may be external (from their instructor) or internal (from their own observations and experience).

femur
The bone that extends from the pelvis to the knee. The femur is the longest and largest bone in the body.

flexion
Any movement that decreases the angle at a joint. Often, this entails bending the knee, hip, and ankle joints simultaneously. See also *extension*.

flexors
The hip muscles, which act to draw the thigh toward the abdomen, and the trunk muscles, which bend the spine forward into a rounded position.

footbed
An insert for shoes or boots designed to support the foot and/or provide a neutral stance.

formal operations stage
The stage of cognitive development that marks the beginning of adult thinking.

frostbite
Freezing or partial freezing of a body part.

frost nip
Cold injury in which only the outer skin layer is frozen. Characterized by pain and blanching of the skin.

generative question
A question designed to provide insight into the values and emotions associated with the answer. "What did you most enjoy about your day on the slopes?" is an example of a generative question. See also *closed question* and *open question*.

goals
The desired lesson outcomes, which the instructor and students agree upon.

hinge joint
A joint in which a convex part of one bone fits into a concave part of another, allowing motion in only one plane. Knee and finger joints are hinge joints.

hypothermia
A dangerous condition in which the body core temperature falls below 95°F. Symptoms include confusion, apathy, withdrawal, and slurred speech.

inertia
The tendency of a body either to remain at rest or to continue in motion in a straight line unless acted on by an external force. The inertia of a body is given by its mass.

inversion
Raising the medial border of the foot and/or a rotation inward of body parts. See also *eversion*.

isometric contraction
Muscle contraction with no change in length. See also *concentric contraction* and *eccentric contraction*.

kinesthetic learning
Learning through feelings and sensations (also known as proprioceptive learning). Kinesthetic refers to forces that act outside the body to create a sensation, such as the boot pressing upon the leg.

lateral
Situated at, proceeding from, or directed toward the side. An upright person who leans to one side moves laterally.

lateral learning
A teaching technique in which the instructor has students focus on a broad range of activities within an ability level so they can experience in-depth learning before progressing to the next level. The instructor helps students isolate and develop skills, integrate them fully, and apply them to various situations before moving to the next level.

learning environment
Conditions affecting the ability to learn.

learning partnership
The rapport the instructor forms with the student. Essential to the success of this relationship is the instructor's understanding of the student's needs and expectations and the student's willingness to actively participate in learning.

learning process
Learning occurs through the steps of readiness to receive information, receiving information, processing, and then reacting to (using) it.

learning style
A person's dominant or preferred mode of learning or processing information. Also known as learning type. One way of classifying learning styles is to determine if a person is primarily a visual, auditory, or kinesthetic learner. Another classification scheme separates types as dynamic learner, innovative learner, active experimenter, or analytical learner. Most people learn through a combination of styles.

lesson planning
The instructor's process of establishing the lesson structure, based on the student goals that the instructor and student have together identified. Lesson duration, snow conditions, student goals, and expectations, and numerous other factors contribute to an effective lesson plan.

ligaments
Bands of thick, strong, fibrous tissue that connect bones and serve to strengthen joints.

mature stage
The final stage of coordination development, when movement becomes relatively well-coordinated, mechanically correct, and efficient.

model
An analogy in which concepts are related to a familiar device or system to facilitate understanding.

modeling
A teaching procedure in which a person demonstrates the correct performance of skills.

momentum
A property of a moving body that is the product of its mass times its velocity.

motor learning
Movements learned by practice or experience that lead to a relatively permanent gain in performance.

movement analysis
The process of assessing a student's ability—the movement patterns and skill blending—and identifying the correlating cause-and-effect relationships. The instructor analyzes the separate components of the student's movements to determine the focus of the lesson and identify the steps that will produce the desired results. Also known as movement assessment.

multiple intelligences
A system for identifying seven comprehensive categories of human capabilities. The multiple intelligences are: verbal-linguistic, logical-mathematical, spatial, bodily-kinesthetic, musical-rhythmic, interpersonal, and intrapersonal.

muscle
Tissue composed of cells that can shorten (contract) and lengthen (relax).

myelin
Covering along pathways linking neurons in the brain and spinal cord. Serves to increase the speed of neural transmission.

Myers-Briggs Type Indicator (MBTI)
Scale that measures individual preferences in thinking and behavior, based on the work of Carl Jung. The types identified include introverted vs. extroverted, sensing vs. intuitive, thinking vs. feeling, and judging vs. perceiving.

National Ski Patrol (NSP)
An association whose members support and participate in the snowsport and outdoor recreation community by providing educational training and emergency care and rescue services.

neuron
Conducting cell of the nervous system.

nordic downhill
Alpine skiing on nordic equipment. The skier may make alpine ski turns as well as telemark turns.

nordic track
Nordic skiing on prepared (groomed) tracks. The skier may use classic technique (traditional diagonal stride) or skate.

objectives
The particular focus a person chooses to reach an overall goal. Objectives pinpoint the actual skills that need to be developed for a goal to be realized. For example, a student must develop progressive edging skills to reach the goal of making rounded turns.

off piste
Terrain that is not on a prepared slope. See also *piste.*

open question
A question that may elicit a broad range of responses. "What did you think about your balance in that turn?" is an open question. See also *closed question* and *generative question.*

pacing
The orchestration of activities that make up a lesson—the intensity of the practice period, its duration, and the frequency of repeating practice.

patella
The kneecap.

pelvis
A cone-shaped bony ring made up of the right and left pelvic bones joined in front and in back.

perceptual motor skills
Motor skills in which perception plays a large role, with perceptual discrimination often dictating appropriate responses.

piste
A European term for a prepared slope. See also *off piste.*

practice
Repetition of movement patterns or other activities designed to develop or refine a skill. Student focus and instructor guidance and feedback are important parts of effective practice.

pre-operations stage
An early developmental stage in which a child begins to use language and to increasingly interact with the world: verbally, mentally, and physically.

previewing
Discussing the basic lesson format with students so they know what to expect.

progressions
A sequence of acts, movements, or events oriented toward meeting an educational objective or goal. Progressions are connected from the least complicated to the most difficult. For example, an edging skill development progression might include side stepping up a hill, then sideslipping, followed by sideslipping to an edge-set.

proprioception
The sense of the position and movements of the body and body parts. Snowsport skill development requires the performer to perceive and use proprioceptive information.

PSIA Demonstration Teams
National teams of the Professional Ski Instructors of America whose purpose is demonstration, teaching, and training across the United States. Member instructors are selected for the teams based on performance and teaching ability. The teams are alpine, nordic, and snowboard.

Q-angle
The angle between the extended axes of the femur and the tibia, measured at mid-patella (kneecap). The angle is typically larger for women than men because women have a relatively wider pelvis.

reinforcement
The process of rewarding students for appropriate performance. Recognizing and praising students for reaching their achievements provides even more motivation to them.

risk management
Using appropriate methods and procedures to reduce risk to customers, guests, and employees at a resort. Instructors, hill employees, management personnel, and volunteers work together to implement area risk management policies.

self-actualization
Developing one's full potential. The highest level of Maslow's hierarchy of needs.

sensorimotor domain
The learning domain related to movement and performance. A beginning and an advanced student can each sense being out of balance. Whereas the motor response of the beginner might be to sit down, the advanced student might respond by adjusting his or her balance to a centered position. See also *affective domain* and *cognitive domain.*

skill
Learned movement, resulting in proficient movement that is controlled, coordinated, and efficient.

skill blending
Combining basic skills to create an overall performance. Expert skiers and riders integrate skills depending on the situation or maneuver. Instructors can evaluate students on their ability to blend and apply skills in a variety of situations.

snow tool
Any of the various sliding tools designed for snowsports, including skis and snowboards.

snowboard
A board for sliding across snow in an angled stance, more like surfing. This device is wide enough to accommodate both feet placed across its width and has characteristics similar to a ski, such a camber and sidecut.

snow types
Approximate classifications of snow. Several types exist:
- *powder*—snow that is light, dry, and fluffy;
- *packed powder*—snow that is pressed together or groomed;
- *corn*—pellet-sized particles that have formed from repetitive thawing, refreezing, and recrystallizing of snow;
- *crud*—settling snow that is cut up by skiers and riders;
- *wind-crust*—snow with a wind-compacted top layer;
- *cement*—uncompacted, heavy snow with a high moisture content;
- *ice*—snow that has become very dense and hard.

spider-webbing
Word exercise designed to stimulate free association in thinking and problem solving.

spine
The bony column that forms the main support for the body and protects the spinal cord. The spine consists of 33 vertebrae.

split
The process of separating a group of students into homogeneous classes. The instructor may group students according to their desired outcomes (e.g., bumps versus groomed conditions), skill level, preferred learning style, student age, or any combination of these variables.

stance
How a skier or rider stands on the snow tool. One of the most basic indicators of performance at all levels of skiing and riding, stance affects the application and blending of skills. The "stacking" of body segments is often best observed from the side.

student-centered teaching
Teaching based on the student's needs, desires, expectations, preferred learning styles, and reactions to the learning process. Student-centered teaching is one of the most fundamental philosophies in ATS.

subtalar joint
Joint between the talus and the calcaneus allowing inversion-eversion movements of the foot.

Sustainable Slopes
Campaign developed by the National Ski Areas Association (NSAA) describing desirable environmental management processes for resorts.

synchronization
Skiers or riders perform tasks and create formations simultaneously, orchestrated with precise timing, rhythm, turn shape, and technique.

tactics
The methods used to gain a desired objective.

task
An assigned activity (e.g., progressing toward a target while maintaining a 20-foot-wide corridor).

teaching for transfer
Drawing upon a student's previous learning to help with present learning, that is, pointing out similarities between familiar movements and new movements. For example, students first learn to create better edge grip for side stepping by rolling their ankles into the hill. Later, students can transfer the movement of rolling the ankles to turning with more edge control.

transfer of learning
Carryover effect of learning in one context to another context.

traverse
Skiing or riding across the slope in a horizontal or diagonal path.

turn shape
The form of the turn arc (the exact path of the skis or board through the turn). The skier or rider creates turn shape with the unique combination of balancing, rotary, pressure control, and edging movements. Turn shape reflects skill level and indicates the timing, intensity, and duration of movements. This should not be confused with turn size.

vestibular system
Ear structures involved with proprioception, providing information about head position in space and sudden changes in direction of body movement.

visual learners
Students who learn best by watching. They prefer demonstrations rather than verbal descriptions or diagrams.

warm-up
A portion of the lesson devoted to preparing for activity. This lesson segment often refers to warming up muscles through light movement and stretching, but instructors also can help students warm up their minds and prepare them to learn through active listening and questioning.

watchers
Another name for visual learners.

windchill
The cooling effect of wind; the coldness felt on exposed skin due to a combination of temperature and wind velocity.

Your Responsibility Code
A code that sets forth the responsibility of each participant for safe conduct on the slopes and lifts. The code comprises seven points and is a partial list of safe conduct with the message to always be safety conscious.

Index

Accommodating, 54
Active experimenters, 14
Adaptive, 82
Aging, 21
Alignment, 80
Altitude, 69
Analytical learners, 13-14
Anatomy, 17
Apathy, 61
Applying learning, 44
Assertiveness, 54
Auditory, 11, 13, 41
Avalanche, 69-70
Avoidance, 54
Behavior, 28
Belonging, 35, 38
Bloom, Benjamin, 44
Bodily-kinesthetic, 14
Body angles, 31
Body language, 26, 40
Bones, 18-19
Brain, 10, 12, 16
Career, 81-84
Center of mass, 20, 32
Certification, 77-78
Children's
    emotional and social
        development, 15-16
    movement assessment, 32-33
    physical development, 20
    teaching, 82
Closure, 39, 45, 48
Coaching
    for students, 24-34
    for self, 77
Collaboration, 54
Communication, 26, 39-40
Competition, 54
Compromise, 54-55
Conditioning, 78-79
Confidence, 25-26
Conflict resolution, 53
Cooperation
Coordination, 20
Customer service, 60-61
Debriefing, 45, 48
Dehydration, 68-69
Demonstration, 39
Describing, 34
Diversity, 81
Doing, 41
Drills, 43
Dynamic learners, 14

Edging, 31
Elementary stage, 20
Emotional factors, 15-16, 26-28
Environmental awareness
    avalanche, 69-70
    climate and weather, 72
    flora and fauna, 73
    mountain environment, 71-74
    summer , 74
    sustainable slopes, 74
Equipment, 32, 79-80
Eversion, 18
Experience, 2, 7, 11-12, 15
Fear, 36-37
Feedback, 34, 42, 44-45, 48
First impression, 26
Fitness, 78-79
Footbeds, 80
Forces, 32
Frostbite, 67-68
Fun, 64
Gardner, Howard, 14
Gender, 22
Goals, 28, 30, 34
Gravity, 20
Group lessons, 42-43
Heirarchy of needs, 35
History of skiing, 2
Human development, 15, 20
Hypothermia, 68
Injuries
    accidents, 71
    altitude-induced, 69
    cold-induced, 67-68
    dehydration, 68
    ultraviolet radiation, 67
Initial stage, 20
Innovative learners, 13
Interpersonal, 15
Intrapersonal, 15
Inversion, 18
Joints, 18-19
Jung, Carl, 28
Kinesthetic, 11-13, 41
Kolb, David, 13
Learning
    activities, 34-44
    and aging, 21
    and emotions, 15-17, 38
    and fear, 38
    and gender, 22
    and performance, 36
    constructing a model, 48

engaging learners, 34
environment, 34, 48
modes, 41
movement skills, 17-20
process, 13
styles, 13, 40
types, 14
Lessons
    group, 42-43
    introduction, 24
    pacing, 67
    preparedness, 67
    previewing, 29
    private, 43
Lifts, 70
Ligaments, 17
Limits, 65
Listening, 26-27, 29
Logical-mathematical, 14
Maslow, Abraham, 35
Mass, 20
Mature stage, 20
Memory, 12, 16-17
Mentor, 7, 81
Metaphor mania, 48
Meyers-Briggs Type Indicator, 28
Modeling learning, 34
Models, 24, 46-48
Momentum, 20
Motivation, 6
Movement assessment, 30-34, 48
Multiple intelligences, 14-15, 41
Musculoskeletal system, 17
Musical-rhythmic, 14-15
Neuron, 10
Participation, 34
Perceptual motor system, 11
Personal mastery, 76
Physics, 19-20
Piaget, Jean, 12
Play, 16
Practice, 42
Previewing, 29
Private lessons, 43
Processing, 13
Professional development, 76
Progressions, 43
Proprioceptive system, 12
Q angle, 22
Questions
    and communication, 40
    closed, 27

generative, 27
in lesson summary, 46
open, 27
Reaction, 13
Readiness, 13
Reception, 13
Reflecting, 41
Relationships, 26, 28, 50
Resort management, 50-53, 60-61
Respect, 56
Risk management, 64-71
Safety
    and learning, 64
    and risk, 64
    and security, 35
    of students, 36
Self-actualization, 35
Self-esteem, 38, 40
Seniors, 82
Sensorimotor system, 11
Sensory, 11, 16
Simile search, 47
Skeletal structure, 18-19
Snow tool, 31
Spatial, 14
Staff, 60
Stance, 31
Subtalar joint, 18
Tangent, 20
Teaching
    activities, 43
    modes, 41
    model, 46-48
    motivation for, 6-8
Teamwork, 50-53
Terrain, 66
Thomas-Kilmann Conflict
    Mode Instrument, 53
Trust, 24-25, 29-30, 48
Turning
    entry, 31
    force, 32
    shape, 31
Ultraviolet radiation, 67
Verbal-linguistic, 14
Vestibular system, 12
Visual, 11, 13, 41
Women, 81
Yikes zone, 38
Your Responsibility Code, 64-65